Sudan: Aid and External Relations

SELECTED ESSAYS

edited by

Mohamed Omer Beshir

GRADUATE COLLEGE PUBLICATIONS
NO 9
UNIVERSITY OF KHARTOUM

First published in 1984 by the Graduate College,
University of Khartoum, PO Box 321
Khartoum Sudan.

General Editor: Mohamed Omer Beshir
Managing Editor: Maureen Makki
Editor of this volume: Mohamed Omer Beshir and
K. Perkins

ISBN0 86372 021 8
Printed & bound in Great Britain by
Biddles Ltd Guildford & King's Lynn
Distributed by Ithaca Press 13 Southwark Street London SE1

CONTENTS

LIST OF CONTRIBUTORS

Mohamed Omer Beshir: Professor of African History, Institute of African and Asian Studies, University of Khartoum.

Guma'a Mohamed Ahmed: Regional Government, Kordofan Province.

Safwat Fanous: Teaching Assistant, Department of Political Science, Faculty of Economic and Social Studies, University of Khartoum.

Abdel Basit Saeed: Department of Political Science, Gezira University.

Salah Khogali Ismail: Sudan Gezira Board.

Omer Mohamed Ali: Department of Political Science, University of Khartoum.

INTRODUCTION

All of the essays in this volume were originally written as chapters of post-graduate theses for the University of Khartoum. Each of them addresses, in one form or another, the question of Sudanese foreign relations. Some examine Sudan's relations with individual neighbors; others look at Sudan in a regional context; while still others take a topical approach, exploring matters, such as economic assistance, which involve Sudan with many other countries. Taken as a whole, the collection offers a good overview of Sudan's place in the international community from its independence in 1956 to the mid-1970s.

Gumaa Mohammed Ahmad's opening essay, "The Sudan: African and Arab", makes the point that Sudan's role as a bridge between the African and Arab worlds is a relatively recent one. He notes the country's traditional orientation to the Arab world, and the failure of early post-independence governments to formulate effective policies towards Africa, with the exceptions of Egypt and Ethiopia which, for historical and geographical reasons, Sudan could not ignore. After 1963, however, when Sudan was one of the founding members of the OAU, a more serious involvement in African affairs began. This new interest in Africa was not unrelated to Sudan's own problems in the south. Efforts to reverse the divisive British colonial "Southern Policy" through enforced Arabization and Islamization in the south were proving counter-productive, and the military government which came to power in 1969 recognized the importance of a peaceful resolution of the crisis which would generate better relations with Black African nations. The Sudan government hoped that those nations would then lend their support as Khartoum proceeded to cope with the difficult period of establishing a new *modus vivendi* with the south.

"Sudan's Role in Afro-Arab Cooperation", by Safwat Fanous, picks up and continues this theme. He observes that the Nimeiri regime's emphasis on "unity in diversity" met with opposition from some Sudanese political leaders who were committed advocates of Arab nationalism. Nevertheless, national survival demanded a change in Sudan's earlier policy of Arabization and Islamization in the south. Moreover, since that policy had had an undeniably negative effect on Afro-Arab relations in general, it was arguable that this new departure would prove an asset to Arabism by facilitating its interaction with African nationalism. The essay underscores Sudan's role as a link between Africa and the Arab world by mentioning the commissions, symposia, and international forums which Sudan has initiated or in which it has been a major participant, whose aim has been to further understanding and promote exchanges between the two communities. Beyond the general advantages of an improved climate of Afro-Arab relations, Sudan has reaped specific and concrete benefits by becoming the recipient of considerable Arab economic aid and a partner in a number of Arab joint investment schemes.

Foreign aid is the subject of two essays by Abdel Basit Saeed. "An Inventory of Foreign Aid to the Sudan" provides a detailed summary of the financial and technical assistance received by Sudan since its independence, with a brief introductory note on pre-independence aid from the Condominium partners, Great Britain and Egypt. Because it analyzes the aid from several perspectives, this paper enables the reader to grasp readily the magnitude of foreign assistance, the amount contributed by various countries and international agencies, and the purposes to which these funds were put. Aid is looked at in terms of multilateral vs. bilateral donors; the political ideologies of donors; and the size of donors' programmes. Separate sections on West German, Italian, and Dutch aid indicate the mechanisms for granting aid, the terms allowed, and the projects funded. These three case studies are used to illustrate the involvement of small, medium, and large donors and the utility of their contributions. Similar portions of the work discuss these same factors with respect to communist donors, Arab donors, and, finally, multilateral agencies.

The second of Abdel Basit Saeed's essays, "Aid from the United States of America and the United Kingdom", offers much the same analytical treatment of the aid relations between Sudan and its two major donors, with the emphasis on American aid. After first discussing the background and purposes of American aid, and pointing out the political nature of the aid process, the author concentrates on American aid to the Sudan under PL 480. He outlines the complex negotiations leading to the initiation of American aid, the terms of the Agricultural Commodities Agreement entered into by the two countries, and a section by section analysis of PL 480 and the ways in which its various clauses have effected Sudan. With reference to the United Kingdom, the mechanics of the aid process are again noted, as are aid terms and the major projects which have resulted from the agreements and loans which the two countries have contracted since the termination of the Condominium.

"American Aid to the Sudan" is also the subject of Salah Khogali's contribution. Less concerned with the details of the aid agreements than the previous author, he recounts the initial opposition of some Sudanese leaders to accepting American aid. He then reviews American aid in the years up to 1969, analyzing its impact on various sectors of the economy and gauging its impact on the country's general development. A similar analysis for the post-1969 years follows. This author agrees that USAID programmes are designed to benefit both donor and recipient, and closes his essay with some comments on how American aid to the Sudan has been closely tied to Americans' perception, at any given time, of Sudan's geo-political importance in the implementation of American policy in the Afro-Arab worlds.

The final essay, by Omer Mohammed Ali, "Sudanese-Egyptian Relations, 1953-1964", looks at Sudan's dealings with its single most important neighbor, and the one with which the country has always been most closely associated. The author notes the Egyptian conviction, which came to change gradually only after the 1952 Revolution, that the only answer to the "Sudan Question" was the latter's total annexation by Egypt. The bulk of this work, however, focuses on the intricate political maneuvering which occurred between 1952 and 1956, as Sudan moved systematically towards self-rule and self-determination. There is a good analysis of the Governor-General's Council, the Electoral Commission, and the

Sudanization Commission, all of which had a considerable bearing on the changing nature of Egyptian-Sudanese relations at the time. The essay closes with a brief review of relations in the post-independence period, pointing out reasons for both countries seeking good relations and the benefits to be dervived by each under such circumstances.

Finally I would like to acknowledge the great help given by Dr K. Perkins of the Department of History, University of South Carolina and his wife Margaret in the preparation of this volume. During Dr Perkin's period as a visiting professor at the Institute of African and Asian Studies, University of Khartoum (1982-83) they both helped considerably with editing, typing and revision. It would not have been possible to produce this volume in its present form without their help. The final responsibility, however, remains with me.

M.O. Beshir

May 1984

THE SUDAN: AFRICAN AND ARAB

By
Gumaa Mohammed Ahmed

INTRODUCTION

During the celebrations of the Sudan's independence in 1956, Ismail al-Azhari, the first Prime Minister of an independent Sudan, proclaimed the guidelines of the country's foreign policy:

> Our government will not betray you as regards the covenants or promises it made and we will not link you with pacts or treaties. We will remain faithful to our neighbours and deal with them in mutual friendship, solidarity, and brotherhood. We will stand as a lighthouse for peace, tranquility, and compassion in this world.[1]

Clearly, a precise foreign policy had not yet taken shape, but the Prime Minister carefully chose such vague terms as "world" and "neighbours", leaving clarifications for a later date. Indeed, the country did not have a Minister of Foreign Affairs until 14 January 1956, when Mubarak Zaroug took up this post. Similarly, the opposition leader, Mohamed Ahmed Mahgoub, did not mention foreign policy in his Independence Day address. In the period immediately preceding independence, the politicians seem to have been completely absorbed in preparations for independence itself, giving little thought to what would happen thereafter. The unique position of the Sudan between the Arab and African states, however, necessitated the formulation of clear-cut policies towards them. The Sudan was a geographical

---

1. Al-Ayyam, 3 January 1956.

projection of the Middle East into sub-Saharan Africa, sharing boundaries with Kenya, Uganda, Zaire, Chad, and the Central African Republic as well as Libya and Egypt.

Accordingly, on 12 January, a committee charged with convening a conference on the Sudan's foreign policy invited sixty prominent Sudanese to discuss the ways and means of preparing a meaningful foreign policy.[2] Among the committee's organizers were Mirghani al-Nasri and Ahmed Mohamed Kheir who suggested the adoption of the declarations of the Bandung Conference as the basic principles of the Sudan's foreign policy. They advocated a policy built around the following principles:

1. The avoidance of treaties or military pacts.
2. The pursuit of an unrestrained policy at the international level, based on the country's interests, aspirations, and goals and not linked to any regional grouping. India, under Nehru's leadership, was the inspiration for this view.
3. To oppose the widespread use of atomic and hydrogen weapons, as they endangered the independence of nations, increased international tension, and could lead to the annihilation of the human race.

Nothing ever came of these recommendations after they were presented to parliament. The members of the committee were, in fact, rather short-sighted in their rejection of regional groupings, for such organizations could strengthen international ties and benefit all the countries concerned.

The first official statement from the Minister of Foreign Afairs came during a visit to Egypt later in January.

The Sudan, in accordance with its position, will try

---

2. Ibid, 12 January 1956.

> to establish and nurture its external relations with the African countries, among which is Ethiopia, and also the Arab countries and those of Bandung.[3]

Ethiopia was singled out for several reasons: the Ethiopian district of Gambeila had been temporarily annexed by the Sudan during the Condominium and the Sudan wished to establish its respect for Ethiopia's frontiers. Moreover, Ethiopia maintained that it should be permitted to enter into any reconsideration of the 1929 Nile Waters Agreement, since the Blue Nile originates on its territory. The Minister continued:

> We will adopt a policy of non-alignment and not join Western or Eastern blocs. We will negotiate with the Egyptian government about foreign policies and means of co-ordination between us. We will not join any bilateral treaties with Arab countries, and regards Israel, we will take the same stand followed by other Arab countries.[4]

These remarks revealed the concern of the Sudanese government with the Arab world, and especially Egypt. The Sudan had already applied for membership of the Arab League and had received unanimous acceptance in an extraordinary meeting on 19 January. The Arab countries were eager to have the Sudan at their side. In order to safeguard its independence and have a voice in

3. Ibid, 24 January 1956.

4. Ibid. At that time there were disputes between some members of the Arab League. King Hussein of Jordan suspected Egypt and Syria of assisting forces bent on overthrowing him. Egypt and Iraq were also competing for hegemony in the Arab world. As a result of these conflicts, each state was trying to win support from other Arab League members through bilateral treaties.

world affairs, the Sudan also applied for membership in the U.N. and was admitted to the world body on 12 November 1956.

The political parties outside the government, as well as other organizations, however, continued to press the government to announce a clear foreign policy. In response, a Ministerial committee was organized, consisting of Mubarak Zaroug (Foreign Affairs), Abdulla Khalil (Defence and Works), Ali Abdul Rahman (Education), Mirghani Hamza (Agriculture and Irrigation), Ibrahim al-Mufti (Commerce and Industry), and Ibrahim Ahmed (Finance). This committee, formed in March 1956, had failed to achieve any results when al-Azhari's government was replaced by a coalition of the Umma Party and the Peoples Democratic Party (PDP) in July 1956. Thus, independent Sudan's first government never managed to lay down meaningful foreign policy principles.

The partners in the new coalition agreed, however, only on the need to exclude al-Azhari from power. They differed among themselves on many issues, not least of which was foreign policy. The Umma Party remembered that Egypt had once discouraged Sudan from opting for independence and, remaining wary of Egyptian aims, opposed any policy of unification between the two countries. The Umma Party also insisted on renegotiating the Nile Waters Agreement of 1929. The PDP, on the other hand, was an old friend of Egypt and supported policies favouring the northern neighbour. At the same time, the PDP accused the Umma of serving the interest of the West, especially the United States and the United Kingdom.

Not surprisingly, this uneasy coalition made no more progress in the field of foreign affairs than its predecessor government. Widespread resentment of its general paralysis led to a military coup on 17 November 1958 under the leadership of General Ibrahim Abboud. This government in turn became preoccupied with economic issues and the increasingly virulent troubles in the south, leaving it little time or inclination to focus on foreign policy matters before it was brought down in 1964. Thus, the Sudan's record in the international field was not particulary notable, even after almost a decade of independence.

ATTITUDE TOWARDS AFRICA

At the beginning of this century the Sudanese identified themselves according to tribes and sub-tribes; one or another of the tariqas, or religious fraternities; inhabitants of a certain region; or as Muslims or Arabs. The latter characterization resulted from the process of Arabization which had been directly linked to Islamization. This indentification is a mark of honour distinguishing them from other, less Arabized, Muslims or non-Muslims. These categorizations continued, in some cases even to the present day, and the term "Sudanese" was rarely used, except with reference to the less sophisticated, non-Islamized and non-Arabized segments of the population.

Under these circumstances, earlier Sudanese writers and poets naturally adhered to the values of traditional Islam and classical Arabic literature, to the almost complete exclusion of their African heritage and environment. In need of psychological reassurance after their humiliation by the Anglo-Egyptian forces, and unable to find it either in the African past or in the realities of contemporary Africa which merely accentuated their feeling of inferiority to the British and Egyptians, they became passionately attached to their heritage, and to Arabic culture and thought. Sudanese politicians tried their best to link the Sudan with the Arab world both before and after independence, however, the Sudanese African past was not a matter for glorification nor was it a source of gratification.

The concept of a Sudanese nationalism able to unite all the people of the Sudan regardless of tribal, religious, or regional differences; foster among them a sense of loyalty to the Sudan as a political entity and a fatherland; and mobilize the Sudanese to achieve independence and socio-economic advancement appeared only after the First World War. Its appearance and growth were greatly influenced by the Sudan's close contact with Egypt's Arabic press and publications; the many Egyptians working in the Sudan; Sudanese merchants and students in Egypt; the example of Egyptian nationalism and the policies of successive Egyptian governments which had claimed that the Sudan was an Egyptian territory and which had aimed, until 1952, at the unity of the Nile Valley under the Egyptian Crown.

Only after independence were the Sudanese compelled to reconsider the nature of their nationalism. This was due mainly to the emergence of the southern Sudanese as active contributors to national politics and the later development of Pan-Arabism and Pan-Africanism as regional forces with a strong appeal to the Sudanese. During the Condominium, the British succeeded in partially screening the Sudan from other African countries. The Sudanese knew very little about Africa because they had to depend on blurred information supplied from time to time by the British press, which viewed Africa as the "Dark Continent" suitable only for exploitation and the humiliation of its people. Azhari's government after independence made no overture to Africa, but Abdulla

Khalil, leader of the government which succeeded it, outlined his policies in the Arab and African spheres in these words:

> I want to make sure that our relations with the Arab countries and especially Egypt are strong and close and will continue so forever. Immediately after acquiring our independence we joined the Arab League in which we will work relentlessly to strengthen relations between its members and to try to co-ordinate their different external policies in all common matters ... As the Sudan is among the very few independent African countries, it shoulders a responsibility towards obtaining freedom for the millions of Africans who are still under colonial rule. We have to turn and look towards Africa.[5]

There had, of course, already been contacts of varying degrees, with some African states, most notably Ethiopia. At the request of the Ethiopian government, independent Sudan returned the district of Gambeila to Ethiopia on 15 June 1956, thereby fulfilling the 1902 treaty stipulating that Gambeila be returned when the Sudan became independent. Prime Minister Abdulla Khalil visited Ethiopia at the invitation of Emperor Haile Selassie in 1957. It was also at this time that Ethiopia sought to participate in the renegotiation of the Nile Waters Agreement, although both the Egyptian and Sudanese governments dismissed the claim at the time.

Problems linked to the rebellion in the southern Sudan after 1955 necessitated contacts between the Sudan and the not yet independent Uganda government. In the spring of 1957 the Uganda government assisted the Sudanese

5. Al-Ayyam, 22 February 1957.

authorities in their search for rebels who were attacking government installations and officials. The Ugandans also agreed to search for rebels who had crossed its borders.

After Ghana's independence the Sudan and Ghana entered into diplomatic relations at the consular level and a Ghanaian delegation visited the Sudan to discuss the All African Conference to be convened by Kwame Nkrumah and Habib Bourguiba.

The government of Abdulla Khalil granted political asylum to six Africans from the British Cameroons when the British authorities expelled them in July 1957. When the refugees requested the government to help them reach the U.N. to present their case there, the Council of Ministers declined and they left for Egypt, whose government had promised to publicise their cause within the Arab world and at the U.N.

The most dramatic plan made by the Sudanese authorities to further their relations with Africa was the Ministry of Communications' 1957 proposal of a huge project to link the Sudan with West and Central Africa by a railway line and an air service. The railway line was to reach Uganda, Kenya, Tanganyika, and Ghana. A delegation composed of the Minister of Communications, the Manager of Sudan Airways, the Manager of Sudan Railways and others flew to Nigeria to discuss the possibility of an air link with that country, but little of the plan ever came to fruition.[6]

Thus, in 1956 and 1957 Sudanese activities in Africa were minimal. The Sudan remained ill-informed about Africa and continued to identify itself primarily with the Arab world. Moreover, the political situation since

6. Al-Ayyam, 6 April, 1957.

independence had been unstable and each government had concentrated more on clinging to power than on formulating external policies.

Sudan's links with the Pan-African movement started seriously when it participated in the Accra Conference of Independent African States in 1958. Mohamed Ahmed Mahgoub, then the Minister of Foreign Affairs, told the conference:

> Divided we are weak and ineffective. But once united in strife, peoples of Africa are capable of immense achievements. However, we must not allow our visions to be blurred by ambition, nor our judgement impaired by greed. We must not betray our sacred trust by substituting fear for freedom and not lighten the burden of the slave to realise that he will exchange for his foreign master one of his own kith and kin.[7]

Sudan's involvement in the conference gave rise to the hope that Sudan might play a more active role in African affairs in the future. This materialized with the formation of the O.A.U. in 1963 with Sudan as a founding member. At the same time, however friendly relations between the Sudan and some African countries began to be eroded as a result of suppressive policies pursued by the military regime in the southern Sudan and its expulsion of foreign Christian missionaries in 1962.

SUDAN: AFRICAN, ARAB, OR BOTH?

The Sudan's ability to identify with both Africa and the Arab world has given rise to much controversy. Many advocates of separation between the northern and southern Sudan have argued that the country could achieve unity

7. Mohamed Ahmed Mahgoub, Democracy on Trial: Reflections on Arab and African Politics (London, 1974), pp. 248-49.

and national integration only by identifying with either Africa or the Arab World, thus implying an inherent conflict between African and Arab states and further suggesting that integration between the Negroid and Arabized Sudanese was impossible. This assertion gives the impression that the Sudan holds the fate of Afro-Arab relations, as well as her own destiny, in her hands and is a focus for Black Africa's latent resentment against northern Africa.[8] Certainly there were, and are, substantial differences between some Sudanese communities, but this does not necessarily preclude cooperation in forming an integrated state associated with both Africa and the Arab World. Those differences were primarily man-made and man-made devises can bring the groups together.[9]

The history of Arabization and Islamization in the northern Sudan has shown that integration naturally results from a system in which people enjoy local autonomy but also interact with others. Such a process gradually transformed the society. In north and central Sudan the indigenous people gradually adopted Islam, beginning in the 7th century, and Arabic systematically replaced the original languages. The Islamization and Arabization of the areas was completed by the early 15th century, as the Arab newcomers married local women, including the daughters of the traditional ruler. This helped solidify their hold, since inheritance in the local tribes traditionally had passed through the females,[10] althouth this custom soon changed to accomodate the Arab practice of

---

8. Mohamed Omer Beshir, <u>The Southern Sudan, Background to Conflict</u> (Khartoum, 1970), p.107.

9. Ibid, p.101.

10. Yusuf Fadl Hasan, <u>The Arabs and the Sudan</u> (Khartoum, 1973), p.127.

inheritance through the male line. Since many of the newcomers represented complete ethnic units, local tribes often claimed Arab ancestry in imitation of the new rulers, giving rise to assertions of Arabness among certain groups. Arabic and Islamic influences did not penetrate the south because of such physical barriers as swamps and thick forests and because of climatic conditions unsuitable to their way of life. It may also be that the Arabs had no desire to Islamize the southern tribes, since doing so would, in view of the Islamic prohibition against enslaving other Muslims, inhibit their slave-trading activities.

While it is difficult to demarcate precisely those parts of the Sudan which experienced Arabization and Islamization, it is possible to divide the country into five regions. In the north-central area live most of the "Arabs", although there are also partially Arabized Nubians. In the north-east are the Beja, non-Arab Muslims. The Nuba Mountains of southern Kordofan province, although part of the northern Sudan, remain the home of the purely African Nubas. The deliberate British policy of aiding Arabization in this area has led to some measure of Islamization.[11] Finally, in the south - the provinces of Equatoria, Upper Nile and Bahr El-Ghazal - there are some 2.8 million Negroid peoples. The concentration of the Arab Sudanese in the north-central heartlands of the Sudan, and their dispersal throughout the country as traders or, in recent years as state officials, resulted in their domination of all spheres of social, economic, and political life.

The British viewed the Sudan largely in terms of the north, and so thought of it as Arab. The concept of two

---

11. Mohamed Omer Beshir, Educational Development in the Sudan, 1898-1956 (Oxford, 1969), pp.72-75.

Sudans - "Southern Policy" - resulted in practically no development in the south, concentrating modernization in the north-central region. Southern Policy played on the cultural differences between the south and north and Christian missionaries worked in the south to win back the confidence of its inhabitants in the government which had been destroyed by the slave trade. The Egyptian government objected to this arrangement, but the Condominium authorities ingeniously answered that the field was open to all who had the desire and the means to work in it, both of which the Muslims evidently lacked.

The 1919 Egyptian Revolution prompted the British to weaken the links between the Sudan and Egypt, creating a further obstacle to the spread of Arab influence and Arab nationalism in the Nile Valley. The British also insisted more vigorously on the separate development of the south, marking a new phase of "Southern Policy". English became the region's lingua franca and southern customs were promoted to the exclusion of all persons and things northern. The Passports and Permits Ordinance of 1922 enabled the British authorities to refuse or withdraw at will permission for non-Sudanese to enter the south or for Sudanese to travel from the north to the south.[12]

Whether or not the British fully realized the long term implications of these policies is arguable, but it is clear that they did contemplate the possibility of eventually linking the south with East Africa. Southern governors did not normally attend the annual meeting of governors, but instead co-ordinated their work, including economic development plans with their colleagues in

---

12. Francis Mading Deng, _Dynamics of Identification, A Basis for National Integration in the Sudan_ (Khartoum, 1973), p.30.

British East Africa. Graduates from southern intermediate schools went to Makerere College in Uganda for higher education. As a result of all this, a sharp division grew between north and south. The Arab Sudanese quite reasonably saw "Southern Policy", especially between 1930 and 1946, as an attempt to detach the south from the north.

Finally, in 1947, under pressure from the northern Sudanese and the Egyptians, Sir James Robertson, the Civil Secretary, declared a policy of unity for the Sudan. In the face of criticism from some British administrators, Sir James insisted that:

> The policy of the Sudan government regarding the Southern Sudan is to act upon the fact that the peoples of the Southern Sudan are distinctly African and Negroid, but geography and economics combine (so far as can be seen at the present time) to render them inextricably bound for their future development to the Middle Eastern and Arabized Northern Sudan.[13]

The signing of the Anglo-Egyptian Agreement on 12 February 1953 was the first major step towards liquidating the Condominium and introducing self-rule and eventual self-determination. The treaty aroused southern political consciousness and the movement there began to take a more coherent shape. It argued that the south had been denied a fair share in the process leading to self-determination, that the constitutional arrangements proposed for the independent Sudan did not sufficiently recognize southern identity, that the unitary system would render the south politically subordinate to the north, and that unity was only possible under a diversified system of government.[14]

---

13. Quoted in Beshir, The Southern Sudan, pp. 62-63.

14. Deng, op cit, p. 370.

Because of the relative backwardness of non-Arab areas, Sudanese Arab politicians monopolized the inicial moves towards self-government. They practically excluded southerners from the pre-independence manouvering, completely ignoring them in the 1952-1953 negotiations in Cairo between Sudanese political parties and Egyptian leaders which compelled the British to accelerate the transfer of power. It was clear that the pattern of British rule and the influence of Egypt on the Sudan's political evolution would make it, in practice, an Arab state, and, indeed, one strongly resistent to the idea of granting concessions to the non-Arabs. After attaining independence, however, the country faced an erosion of national loyalty and the rise of such strong particularistic tendencies that regional loyalties have often equalled or surpassed national sentiment.[15]

Northern Sudanese responded to the "Southern policy" after independence by redoubling their efforts to recover lost ground and to strengthen their position and that of Arab culture in the south. Towards this end they promoted a new policy of Arabization and Islamization intended to counteract the separatist policy of the British. With an eye towards cultural integration, the government unified the educational system and nationalized all missionary schools in the south. In 1964 foreign christian missionaries were expelled from the south. General Abboud's memorandum on this action explained that:

---

15. Muddathir Abd Al-Rahim, 'Arabism, Africanism and Self-Identification', in Sudan in Africa, ed. by Yusuf Fadl Hassan (Khartoum University Press, 1971), p.228.

> It had been proved beyond doubt that the British policy in the Sudan was moving towards a separate southern entity. Conditions in the South lend themselves to the achievement of this goal. The missions were well suited to work for separation. Their influence and moral power were undisputed. Differences in tribal outlook, culture, language and belief among the Southern people were effectively exploited by them for their purpose. In 1929 the Governor-General had given the signal for this policy to be adopted. He stated in his annual report "Missions are our bulwark against Islam in the Sudan".[16]

A department of Religious Affairs was created to organize and supervise Islamic institutes and to merge Islamic and other academic studies.[17]

These attempts at Islamizing and Arabizing the south by simply reversing British policy did not, of course, solve the problem. Their advocates failed to take into account the manner in which Arabization and Islamization had occurred in the north or the history of slavery and other factors of hostility to the north in the south. Nor did they appreciate the repercussions of suddenly reversing a policy which had strong roots in the south, particularly among the educated class. The policy of forced integration only widened the cleavage between the two regions until the situation reached a climax with the emergence, in 1963, of the Anya Nya guerillas who were committed to a military solution.

The northern political parties also failed to give sufficient weight to the undeniable differences between the regions. A special commission formed in 1956 listed

---

16. Quoted in Deng, p. 38.
17. Ibid.

a number of points which it urged all Sudanese to bear in mind so as to understand the 1955 southern revolt which began a period of civil violence which continued for over sixteen years. The commission made its points in five broad categories:

1. Northern and southern Sudanese have very little in common. Racially, the north is Arab: the south Negroid. Religiously, the north is Muslim: the south pagan. Linguistically northerners speak Arabic: southerners some eighty languages . In addition to these factors, there are geographical, historical, and cultural differences.
2. For historical reasons southerners regard northern Sudanese as traditional enemies.
3. British administrative policy until 1947 encouraged the southern Sudanese to progress along African and Negroid lines. Through the Closed Districts Order and the Permits of Trade Order the Sudanese were prevented from knowing each other or learning from each other. The missionaries, who controlled much of the education system in the south, favoured this policy for reasons of their own.
4. For political, financial, geographic, and economic reasons the northern Sudan progressed quickly in every field, while the southern Sudan lagged behind. This inevitably created a feeling among the under-developed people that they were being cheated, exploited, and dominated.
5. All of these circumstances contributed to the absence among the southern Sudanese of a feeling of common citizenship with the northern Sudanese or a feeling of nationalism or patriotism towards the Sudan as a whole. Their loyalty remained tribal.[18]

18. Ibid, p.102.

Many southern Sudanese actively participated in national politics after the termination of "Southern Policy" in 1946. As products of that policy, they were usually bitter and hostile towards their northern compatriots. Large numbers of them, including many graduates of the missionary schools, regarded themselves as a different nation from the northerners and advocated their own independent state or, if some link with the north were inevitable, a weak federal arrangement.

Despite their grievances, the southerners ultimately supported independence on the basis of northern promises that their call for a federal system would receive full consideration. After independence, however, the idea was rejected. Southerners did not object to the principles of cross-cultural assimilation and national unity, but rather to the way in which northerners viewed these ideas. The effort to maintain and spread Arabic culture required the retention of political and economic control in the hands of Arab Sudanese. Under the parliamentary system after independence, many non-Arabs, such as the Beja, challenged this notion. The growing resentment of the east, the west, and the south and the increasing assertiveness of their spokesmen were beginning to have an impact at the time of the overthrow of the parliamentary system in 1969.[19]

Free and fair elections coupled with expanding education in rural areas had begun to produce results which had taken the form of threatening regional pressures.

---

19. Oluwadare Aguda, "Arabism and Pan-Arabism in Sudanese Politics", in Journal of Modern African Studies, Vol. 11, No. 21, 1973, p.186.

The growing insistence in the north from 1967 to 1969 on the adoption of an Islamic constitution for the Sudan came partly as a reaction to the shifting balance of political forces and partly in an attempt to obstruct mounting communist influence. Every northern political party, except for the Communists, agreed to the call for an Islamic constitution.[20] Plans for such a document greatly disturbed southerners and the Nuba, all of whom feared most that it would confirm their status as second class citizens and enable the northerners to monopolise political control indefinitely.[21]

Since Arabic is not the mother tongue of the majority of the population, its adoption as the country's official language clearly stemmed from nationalist motives. Certainly it satisfied the Arabs' self-esteem and strengthened their hold on the state apparatus and economy. Discrimination in public employment and in promotion, allegedly because of a poor knowledge of Arabic, has caused much bitterness among southern Sudanese. Commenting on the demand of the southern members of the Constitutional Committee that English be recognized as a second official language, the conservative daily El-Rai el-Aam expressed surprise that anyone was "opposing Arabic as the official language of the state ... We do not want our native language to be shared by any others.[22] Northerners generally treated requests for separate cultural development with contempt and intolerance. Consequently, the least "Arab"

---

20. See the memorandum submitted to the Constituent Assembly by the National Committee for the Constitution, as quoted in The Vigilant, Khartoum, 12 December 1968.

21. Khartoum News Service, 5 February 1968.

22. Ibid, 3 February 1968.

segments of the population have rejected, often violently, the notion of the Sudan evolving into an Arab cultural nation, since it entailed cultural assimilation and was perceived as a guarantee of their economic and political inequality. Arab Muslim culture, seen by northerners as an integrative factor, became a symbol of suppression for southerners and other non-Arabs. Power struggles ensued between the north and the south on one hand, the north, the east and west on the other.

The question of Sudan's identity and its relations with the Arab world became an issue in Sudanese political life when Arab nationalism assumed new dimensions under the leadership of Jamal Abdel Nasser.[23] Arab nationalism stood not only for Arab unity but also served as a shield against imperialism and a device to achieve victory over Israel. An alliance developed between Arab nationalism and socialism which educated youth in the Arab world increasingly supported. The northern Sudanese identified the Sudan with the Arab world, but thought of Arabism in these terms rather than in racial ones.[24] At the same time, African nationalism concentrated on achieving political independence, since most African countries were still under colonial rule. Not until the 1960s did the concepts of pan-Africanism and African unity dominate the continent's political thinking.

The nationalist movement in the Sudan had little contact with independence movements elsewhere in Africa. The country's relations with the rest of Africa became an issue in Sudanese politics only after it joined the OAU in 1963. Yet the southern Sudanese never ceased to consider themselves different from the northern Sudanese

---

23. Beshir, The Southern Sudan, p.135.
24. Ibid.

or to identify themselves more with African problems and themes than with Arab ones. Many argued that they had far more in common with East Africa than with the Arab world, particularly racially and culturally. Moreover, "people from the same tribes live on both sides of the borders of the Sudan with Uganda, Kenya, Zaire and Ethiopia ... The majority of the political leaders in these regions are Christian and English-speaking."[25]

One result of this identity crisis in the Sudan was the misuse of the terms "Arabism" and "Africanism". In the popular mind they indicated only certain racial groups and were therefore, regarded as mutually exclusive. Thus, "Arabism" was perceived to relate only to the north, while "Africanism" could only refer to the south and its Negroid population. This misusage widened the gap between Arabised and non-Arabised sections of the society.

Dr. Muddathir Abdel Rahim has defined "Arabism" as follows:

> Arabism is a cultural, linguistic, and non-racial link that binds together numerous races: black, white, and brown. Had Arabism been anything else but this, most modern Arabs, whether African or Asian, including the entire population of the Northern Sudan, would cease to be Arabs at all.[26]

It is, however, indisputable that the term "Arabism" does involve certain racial assumptions. If it did not, a Nuba or southern Sudanese Muslim, each culturally Arabized and speaking Arabic, might be called an "Arab" despite his Negroid and pagan ancestry. Dr Muddathir went on to define "Africanism".

---

25. Ibid, p.136

26. Muddathir Abd Al-Rahim, op cit.

> Africanism also is geographical, political, and cultural, but is a non-racial link which links together the various peoples of Africa irrespective of differences of race, colour or language.[27]

These definitions help to explain how Arabism and Africanism developed a strong affinity in the northern Sudan and why the great majority of the population there feel they are Arabs and Africans to an equal degree and without any sense of contradiction. That they are predominantly Muslim and Arab distinguishes them from their southern compatriots but does not cancel their Africanness. In Sudan the physical, racial, and cultural diversities of Africa as a whole are not merely represented but have been synthesized into a unique entity.[28]

Nevertheless, both Arabic speakers in the north and southerners have all occasionally exaggerated the ethnic chasm separating them. The remarks of Aggray Jaden, the president of SANU, at the March 1965 Khartoum Conference on the southern Sudan offer a case in point. He declared that:

> The Sudan falls into two distinct areas, both in geographical area, ethnic groups, and cultural systems. The Northern Sudan is occupied by a hybrid Arab race who are united by their common language, common culture, and common religion, and they look to the Arab world for their cultural and political inspiration. The people of the Southern Sudan, on the other hand, belong to the African ethnic group of East Africa. They do not only differ from the hybrid Arab race in origin, arrangement, and basic systems, but in all

---

27. *Ibid*.
28. *Ibid*.

> conceivable purposes. There is nothing in common between the various sections of the community, no body of shared beliefs, no identity of interests, no local signs of unity and, above all, the Sudan has failed to compose a single community.[29]

Jaden said this despite the fact that the 1955-56 census had estimated that of Sudan's thirteen million people, 30% were southerners, 13% western, 12% Beja and Nuba, 3% Nubian, nearly 40% Arabs, and the rest foreigners or miscellaneous groups.[30]

The maintenance of the two ethnic personalities - "Arab" and "Negro" - within a single territorial entity should, however, be the aim of every Sudanese, because they constitute the most important point of contact between Arab Africa and Black Africa. As evidence of this there is the phenomenon of racial mixture and intermarriage in the northern Sudan and the fact that many Arab Sudanese are, in fact, Arabized Negroes rather than ethnically Semitic. For many of them Arabness is a cultural acquisition, not a racial heritage. Thus, it is the Sudanese, more than any other group, who have given the Arabs a decisive "Negro" dimension in this racial sense.[31] W.E.B. Dubois, the father of Pan-Africanism, observed:

---

29. George W. Shepherd, Jr., "National Integration and the Southern Sudan", in <u>Journal of Modern African Studies</u>, Vol. 4, No. 2, p.195.

30. O. Aguda, "Arabism and Pan-Arabism in Sudanese Politics", in <u>Journal of Modern African Studies</u>, Vol. II, No. 21, p.186.

31. Ali A. Mazrui, "The Multiple Marginality of the Sudan", <u>in Sudan in Africa</u>, p.243.

> Anyone who has travelled in the Sudan knows that most of the "Arabs" he has met are dark skinned, sometimes practically black, often have negroid features, and hair that may be almost Negro in quality. It is then obvious that in Africa the term "Arab" is often misleading. The Arabs were too nearly akin to Negroes to draw an absolute colour line.[32]

In the northern Sudan, Islam and Arabic culture precipitated a high degree of integration. According to Yusuf Fadl Hasan, Islam assisted in the creation of a feeling of cohesion among the heterogeneous inhabitants of the country and its gradual absorption into the Arab world.[33]

On the other hand, relations between the northern and southern Sudan constituted one of the most acute crises in Africa until the Addis Ababa Agreement of 1972 ended the seventeen year old conflict, at least temporarily. For years it had seemed as if an inconclusive civil war would be a permanent aspect of Sudanese politics unless the unstated requirement that Arabism was the sine qua non for enjoying the full rights of citizenship was either abandoned by the Arab Sudanese or accepted by everyone else. In early 1972 the conflict ended abruptly when the government of President Nimeiri granted the south substantial political autonomy and cultural self-determination.

From the time Nimeiri took office in May 1969, his wish was to solve the conflict by means other than war, but the pan-Arab emphasis of the early days of his regime was too strong to allow a truly conciliatory atmosphere

---

32. W.E.B. Dubois, The World and Africa (New York, 1965), p.184.

33. Hasan, op cit, p.181.

to emerge. This alienated the non-Arabs and strengthened the southerners' long-standing distrust of northern intentions regarding their political demands. After large scale demonstrations in Khartoum in support of the official declaration of autonomy in 1969, southern leaders expressed their scepticism to the Revolutionary Command Council, saying:

> The Southerners have not only ceased to have faith in promises any more, they actually believe that these promises are stratagems with which to destroy the legitimate rights of the citizens in the South.[34]

In August 1969, Nimeiri's three month old government announced that it had uncovered a revolt by a group calling itself the "Free Negroes Movement". Government officials referred to those involved in it as "racialist conspirators", a term of opprobrium in Sudanese political vocabulary. The phrase refers to regional agitators, indicating that regional movements had a reality and had reached a serious stage at this time. Many were arrested and tried, including the Reverend Philip Abbas Ghaboush, the Nuba Mountains' leader in the 1968 parliament, who was sentenced to death in absentia.

Apparently a widespread, but poorly organized, anti-government movement with support in the south, the Nuba mountains, and the west was germinating even before Nimeiri came to power. Inspiration for this conspiracy was the political domination and economic neglect from which these areas suffered. But it was the new regime's strong pan-Arab pronouncements which triggered the revolt. On taking power, Nimeiri said:

> The people have expressed their wish to see the Sudan

34. Aguda, op cit, p.196.

> take its rightful place among Arab and African Revolutionary forces, They want to be externally linked with the Arab nation and to support the rights of the people of Palestine.[35]

The new Prime Minister, Babiker Awadalla, went on to observe that:

> The revolutionary government, with complete understanding of the bond of destiny and the forces of the Arab Revolution, will work for the creation of economic, military, and cultural relations with brother Arab nations to strengthen the Arab nation in its fight against neo-colonialism and Zionism ... As for the U.A.R., which is part of us and which is bound to us by the unity of land, blood, history, language, suffering, and aims, it will occupy a special and marked position in our relations with the Arab world.[36]

Two years later, after considerable violence and uncertainty, there was a dramatic switch in policy as Nimeiri decided to concentrate on solving Sudanese internal conflicts before contemplating union with other Arab states. The granting of substantial autonomy to the south tilted the political balance in the country against Arabism and pan-Arabism. The new terms contrasted markedly to the policy of southern autonomy announced in June 1969, which had fallen far short of what militant southerners would accept. In any event, the Anya Nya leadership had not been consulted in 1969, nor was the pan-Arab government of the time in a position to implement any meaningful concessions for the south.

Although most Arab Sudanese have generally opposed

---

35. Sudan News, 26 May, 1969.
36. Ibid.

the idea of merger with Egypt, primarily for historical and economic reasons, there has always been a strong pro-Cairo group, and it is not surprising that Nimeiri's change of emphasis alienated some of his colleagues.[37] Nonetheless, the issue of national integration continued to dominate Sudanese politics, and despite the Addis Ababa Agreement there were still conflicts over Arabism in the Sudan, as shown in the Jonglei canal incident in October 1974, and the Akobo Crisis of March 1975. The first of these involved serious demonstrations in Juba by rioters who believed that the area of the Jonglei canal would be occupied by the Egyptians. The second event cost the lives of twelve northern soldiers and a southern officer because of the erroneous belief that an unscheduled integration of northern and southern soldiers was about to occur. The management of affairs in the southern Sudan remained a most delicate matter.

Nothing, however, could change the fact that the Sudan was both "African" and "Arab". In this identity, it differs even from those Sudanic states which it most

---

37. The Minister of Defence, Khalid Hassan Abbas, who was also Commander in chief of the Army, resigned both appointments and was soon followed, "for health reasons", by the First Vice-President Babiker Awad-Alla, who had previously been Prime Minister. Then Mamoun Awad Abu Zeid, Abul Ghasim Hashim, and Zein Elabdin Mohamed Ahmed Abdel Gadir were released from their ministerial responsibilities. All these people were believed to be supporters of a link with Egypt. For unknown reasons, Khalid Hassan Abbas and Mamoun Awad Abu Zeid were reinstated in July 1975 as members of the Political Bureau and advisors to the President for African and Arab Affairs respectively. Before that Zein Elabdin had also been reappointed to the Political Bureau and named Minister for Youth. In September 1975, Abul Ghasim Hashim rejoined the Political Bureau and became a Commissioner for Gezira Province.

resembles. All the Sudanic states (Somalia, Chad, Niger, Mali, Nigeria, Senegal, and Mauritania) form a bridge between "Arab", or North, Africa and "Black", or sub-Saharan, Africa and all experience tensions between their predominantly Islamic northern regions and their heavily "pagan" or Christian southern regions, but none of them can be said to constitute "an Arab-African entity in the same sense or to the same degree as the Sudan".[38] Many African countries have experienced ethnic cultural conflicts similar to the Sudan's but the latter's case was sufficiently different to lead Professor Ali Mazrui to say:

> The fascination of the Sudan lies in her profound intermediacy as she compulsively absorbs into her being a diversity of traits. Parts of Africa which are otherwise vastly different have been known to experience a moment of self-recognition as they cast their eyes on the Sudan.[39]

The Addis Agreements attained a measure of peace and unity in the southern Sudan, but the difficult and dangerous question of integration remained to be tackled. Dr Deng urged that it be dealt with cautiously.

> If one's objective is to assimilate culturally and thereby alter the identity of another group, a strategy which does not threaten the usurpation of that group's power over its own affairs, but which fosters symbols of the favoured identity, promises better results.[40]

---

38. Hasan, op cit, p.228.
39. Mazrui, op cit, p.254.
40. Deng, op cit, p.2.

The southern Sudanese could hardly have been expected to content themselves only with regional participation and show no concern over major national and international issues affecting Sudan's identity. As Africa moved towards unity and close association, no African state claiming to follow modern policies could base itself on racial or cultural homogeneity.

The vigorous reactions in the UN and the OAU against policies of racial discrimination and apartheid in Rhodesia and South Africa would render ludicrous any effort by the Sudan to justify allowing itself to be divided into two or more parts according to racial differences. Mohamed Omer Beshir has written:

> Thus the politics of Afro-Arab cultural conflict and harmony are not exclusively the burden or concern of Sudan; but in the case of the Sudan they have been magnified, and in some cases exaggerated.

The same author also says:

> In fact Pan-Arabism and Arab aspirations are not contradictory to Pan-Africanism and African aspirations. The majority of those who describe themselves as Arabs - 60 per cent - live in Africa. They are involved in the problems of the continent as much as those who describe themselves as Africans. The past divisions between Arab Africa and Non-Africa, between Islamic Africa and non-Islamic Africa, between Black Africa and non-Black Africa and Africa and between Africa north of the Sahara and Africa south of the Sahara are disappearing fast. New concepts of Pan-Africanism and African unity and co-operation are replacing these concepts which have, in the past, led to conflicts. Pan-Africanism can hardly be distinguished today from revolutionary Pan-Arabism.[41]

41. Beshir, The Southern Sudan, From Conflict to Peace, pp.137-138.

SUDAN'S ROLE IN AFRO—ARAB COOPERATION

By

Safwat Fanous

Successive Sudanese governments up to 1969 generally believed that the solution to the southern problem lay in achieving integration through enforced Arabization and Islamization, particularly of the non-Arab Sudanese. This attitude damaged the Afro-Arab character of Sudan and provoked a resentment of Arab culture which was so strong among some southerners that they went to the extreme extent of enlisting support from Israel. The southerners also propagandized in Black Africa against what they labelled as "Arab imperialism", thus fostering a Black African mistrust of Arab Sudanese governments. Overall, Sudan contributed negatively to Afro-Arab relations in the 1960s.

In March 1972, however, the Nimeiri government and the Southern Sudan Liberation Front signed the Addis Ababa Agreement ending the civil war in the south. The south then had its own Regional Government and People's Assembly; the Anya-Nya were absorbed into the Sudanese armed forces and all such regional activities as education, transportation, agriculture, and health services became the responsibility of regional bodies.

As a prelude to the Addis Ababa Agreement, a significant policy change occurred. For the first time since independence, the Sudanese government admitted that Sudan was composed of diverse cultural and ethnic groups. Acting on the slogan "Unity in Diversity", the May regime abandoned Arabization and Islamization as means of achieving national unity. The government recognized the historical and cultural differences between the north and south and firmly believes that the unity of our country must be built upon these objective realities. The Southern People have the right to develop their respective cultures and traditions within a united Socialist Sudan".[1] In a speech in Wau on the third anniversary of the Regional Self-Government Act, President Nimeiri again stressed this concept, and its importance for the whole of the continent, saying:

> Unity based on diversity has become the essence and the raison d'etre of the political and national entity of many an emerging African country today. We take pride in the fact that the Sudan of the Revolution has become the exemplary instance of this new hope. The Sudan is the biggest country in Africa. It lies in its heart and at its crossroads. Its extensive territory borders eight African countries. Common frontiers mean common ethnic origins, common cultures, shared ways of life, and environmental conditions. Any serious trouble in the Sudan would, of necessity, spill over its frontiers, and vice versa.[2]

The seventeen year civil war and the Addis Ababa Agreement each in its own way dramatized the Afro-Arab nature of Sudan. After 1972, a new policy based upon the "marginality of the Sudan - Arab and African, Islamic,

---

1. Democratic Republic of the Sudan, Ministry of National Guidance, Cultural Section. Policy statement on the Southern Question. (Khartoum, June 6, 1969), p.2.

2. Ministry of Information. Text of Address given by H.E. Gaafar Mohammad Nimeiri, President of the D.R. of the Sudan, on the occasion of the National Unity Day, Wau, 3 March 1975. (Khartoum, 1975).

Christian and animist, black and brown"[3] developed.

As a step towards solving the southern problem, Nimeiri had, since coming to power, paid more attention to Africa than his predecessors. He called a summit meeting in Khartoum in January 1970 which Burundi, the Central African Republic, Chad, Congo-Brazzaville, Zaire, Ethiopia, Kenya, Malawi, Somalia, Rwanda, Tanzania, Uganda, and Zambia attended. A policy of normalizing Sudan's relations with its neighbours and participating more in African politics ensued. Indeed, the mediation efforts of Ethiopian Emperor Haile Selassie, the World Council of Churches, the All African Council of Churches and representatives of Ghana and Liberia, have prompted some writers to describe the Addis Ababa Agreement as an "African solution".[4]

When Egypt, Libya and Syria proclaimed the Federation of Arab Republics in September 1971, Sudan refused to join, despite its adherence to the Tripoli Charter which lay at the root of the new federation. At the time, the Nimeiri government was holding secret negotiations with the southerners to end the war and feared that the political forces rising to power in the south would not accept such strong involvement in the Arab World. Southerners feared the prospects of increased Arab influence and domination in the Sudan the very situation against which they fought. For Nimeiri himself, this act was a

> ratification of something he had begun increasingly to feel: that the future of the Sudan lay in its role as a bridge between the two areas, and not in

---

3. R.P. Stevens, "The 1972 Addis Ababa Agreement and Sudan's Afro-Arab Policy", in Journal of Modern African Affairs, Vol.14, No.2, June 1976, p.249.

4. Ibid., p.253.

membership in either.[5]

Internally, Arab nationalists such as Khalid Hassan Abbas, the Vice-President and Minister of Defence; Babiker Awadallah; Mamun Awad Abu Zied; and Mohieddin Sabir lost their positions in 1972 because of their opposition to the new policy. Nimeiri replaced them with men whom T.C. Niblock has called "Pragmatists - people with academic background holding distinguished academic qualifications", including Jaafar Mohammad Ali Bakheit, Mansour Khalid, Bashir Abbadi, Abdulla Abdel Rahman, and Wadie Habbashi. They together with the southerners, emerged as the new political force.[6]

These events strained Sudan's relations with Egypt, Libya, and Syria from 1972 to 1974, Sudanese troops stationed at Suez were recalled and the Egyptian owned Khartoum Branch of the Nasr Trading Company was closed.[7] In an interview in the Cairo weekly Akhbar al-Yom the Sudanese Ambassador denied accusations that Sudan had turned its back on the Arab World.[8] Before flying to Khartoum to attend the Revolution's third anniversary celebrations, Colonel Qaddafi released a statement that "the Sudanese people were of ethnic Arab stock and that the Addis Ababa Agreement was an attempt to Africanize the Sudan".[9]

---

5. J. Bulloch, The making of a War (London, 1974), p.124.

6. T.C. Niblock, "A new Political System in the Sudan", in African Affairs, Vol. 73, No. 293, October 1974, p.415.

7. Sudanow, Vol. 1, No. 12, December 1976, p.11.

8. Arab Report and Record, 1973, p.15.

9. Sudanow, Vol.1, No. 7, July 1976, p.8.

The policy of stressing the Sudan's Afro-Arab nature even found a place in the country's Permanent Constitution. In debating the Draft Constitution, Omer al-Hag Musa noted that "initially Article One stated that Sudan was part of the Arab World". With the reconciliation of the north and the south, he continued, the phrase "and part of Africa" should be added. Eventually the committee responsible for drafting the Constitution settled on the phrase "part of both the Arab and African entities".[10] In the same debate, Sayed Aldo Ajo Deng observed that "for a long period in the past this country connected itself with Arab Governments. Hence, Sudan was known as one of the Arab countries at a time when we wanted to feel that we were Africans".[11] After discussing the wording of the proposed Article, the entire Assembly agreed to the following formula:

> The Democratic Republic of the Sudan is a unitary, democratic, socialist and sovereign republic, and is part of both the Arab and African entities.[12]

That the old policy of stressing the Arab nature of Sudan at the expense of its African character was no longer acceptable was a by-product of the Addis Ababa Agreement.

The Permanent Constitution's emphasis on building a secular rather than a religious state, and thus again stressing the marginality of the Sudan, also stemmed from the Agreement. In debating the Draft Constitution, some representatives suggested adding to Article One

---

10. Discussions of the First People's Assembly, Meeting No. 79, 11 March 1973, p.39.

11. Ibid., p.41.

12. The Permanent Constitution of the Sudan, (Khartoum, 1973), p.2.

the phrase "part of the Islamic entity", but the north-south reconciliation prompted the Assembly to exclude this phrase. Another proposal for an article stating that "Islam is the official religion of the state" also failed to win the required two-thirds majority for passage. In the words of Jaafar Mohammad Ali Bakheit,

> We want to build a state based on citizenship and not on religion. Loyalty should be to the Sudanese soil and not to religion. If the country adopts a religion for itself then it will be connected to something that does not unite all the Sudanese. This issue was a source of suspicion between the North and the South in the past and we do not want to raise this suspicion again.[13]

In addition, English achieved recognition as the priciple language in the southern provinces. All these developments reflected the southerners' growing influence and their active participation in the regime. The days when the Arab Sudanese dominated the country's political scene were over and the Afro-Arab nature of Sudan could no longer be degraded or ignored.

Sudanese foreign policy also came to emphasize this Afro-Arab character. Addressing the Central Committee of the SSU on 6 March 1975, President Nimeiri said:

> It is the fate of the Sudan and the Sudanese people to be an inalienable part of the Afro-Arab entity. If conditions of disunity and humiliation in the past and defunct regimes prevented our country from contributing to the Arab and African fields of struggle, the present day Sudan responds to the call of affiliation and the call of destiny in fulfilment

---

13. Proceedings of the First People's Assembly, Meeting No. 82, 14 March 1973, pp. 24-26.

> of its national responsibility towards our Arab Nation and our mother continent.[14]

Bona Malwal (then Minister of State for Information), addressing a gathering of African journalists in Nairobi in 1975, said that a Sudanese was "never content to be identified only as an Arab or only as an African, and never ready to give up either his Arab role or his African role".[15] In an interview with African journalist Raph Uwechue, Nimeiri said of Sudan's Afro-Arab role:

> The strength of our position as both African and Arab lies in the fact that neither of the two can deny our presence with them. In that sense we are the richest nation in that region in terms of belonging.[16]

Arabism and Africanism had clearly ceased to be contradictory forces within the Sudan. As Francis Deng put it: The South-North domestic conflict was a thorn in relations between the Africans and the Arabs, but the settlement of the problem was equally an Afro-Arab victory.[17] The great significance of the Addis Ababa Agreement was in preparing the way for the Sudan to play a positive role in Afro-Arab cooperation.

Sudan's contribution to Afro-Arab Cooperation

The initiative for Afro-Arab cooperation had come from Black Africa, beginning with the formation of the Committee of Seven, headed by Sudan, to contact Arab oil producing countries in search of preferential oil

---

14. _Sudan News Agency Bulletin_, (7 March 1975), p.2.
15. _Sudan News Agency Bulletin_, (11 February 1975), p.4.
16. _Africa_, No. 83, July 1978, p. 17.
17. _Sudanow_, Vol. 1, No. 6, June 1976, p.21.

prices. Sudan's major contribution to Afro-Arab cooperation was its advocacy of the concept, which it took as a primary responsibility. In 1974 Nimeiri told a conference of Sudanese ambassadors it was their duty to work for the promotion of Afro-Arab solidarity and cooperation.

The Sudanese newspapers, al-Sahafa and al-Ayyam were the two Arab publications which devoted the most space to Afro-Arab cooperation, as the table below, enumerating articles on Afro-Arab relations in some Arabic papers between 1973 and 1976, shows,[18]

Name of Newspapers	Number of Articles
al-Ayyam (Sudanese)	69
al-Sahafa (Sudanese)	80
al-Ahram (Egyptian)	70
al-Akhbar (Egyptian)	40
al-Thawar (Iraqi)	16
al-Taakhi (Iraqi)	-
al-Watan (Kuwaiti)	4
al-Siasa (Kuwaiti)	-

Following the October War, the two Sudanese newspapers started a campaign urging OAPEC to give special oil prices to Black African countries on the grounds that these states had shown solidarity with the Arabs by severing diplomatic relations with Israel. The two dailies again called attention to the unique position of Sudan, whose role in these events they made very clear, as a link between Arabs and Africans.[19]

---

18. Awatif Abdel RAhman, "Africa and Arab Public Opinion", in E. Kheiri, Ed., Afro-Arab Relations: An Analytical Study (Cairo, 1976), p.537.

19. Ibid., p.531.

In November 1973, Nimeiri, a Muslim, acted as spokesman for a delegation consisting of Emperor Haili Selassie (Christian Orthodox), a representative of the Liberian President (Christian Protestant) and a representative of the Zambian President (Christian Catholic) which visited Rome and had an audience with Pope Paul VI to discuss the future of the Holy City of Jerusalem. Nimeiri expressed Africa's concern over Israel's continuing occupation of Jerusalem. The delegation won a declaration from the Vatican calling for an Israeli withdrawal from the Holy City.[20]

An Afro-Arab Symposium for Liberation and Development met in Khartoum early in 1976 in response to a call from the Sudan. More than eighty delegates from twenty-four Arab and African countries, including the Secretary-General of the Arab League, a representative of the OAU Secretary General, a representative of the Unesco General Director, a number of Arab and African information ministers, and several distinguished Arab and African scholars, attended. The symposium, which was the first serious attempt to give a scientific and scholarly dimension to the Afro-Arab cooperation movement, discussed such subjects as Afro-Arab liberation, racial discrimination, development and economic cooperation, and cooperation between the Arab League and the OAU. President Nimeiri and other dignitaries who addressed the symposium all emphasized its importance in crystallizing Afro-Arab solidarity in working towards common goals.

As a prelude to the 1978 Khartoum International Fair, an Afro-Arab trade symposium opened in Khartoum in January of that year. The Sudanese, Arab, African, and European businessmen who participated discussed

---

20. Al-Sahafa, Khartoum, 22 December 1973, p.l.

promoting trade and the possibility of establishing joint Afro-Arab institutions similar to those of the European Economic Community. After drawing attention to the low level of trade between Black African and Arab countries, the symposium recommended lifting customs barriers and setting up free trade zones, as well as urging greater Afro-Arab cooperation in establishing joint ventures in tourism and industry, especially agro-industry, some of them to be financed by an Afro-Arab bank created for this purpose.[21]

The Institute of Afro-Asian Studies of the University of Khartoum, the first Arab or African academic institute to give special emphasis to Afro-Arab Cooperation, organized an Afro-Arab symposium at Sharqa in 1976, underscoring the tendency of the Arab countries to turn to Sudan when they wanted to deal with Black Africa. Conversely, when the OAU formed Committee of Seven to contact the Arab League, it chose Sudan to head it, presumably because "the African countries understood Sudan and accepted it more than the white Arab African countries".[22] Although the Committee failed to get preferential oil prices for the Black African countries, it did draw OPEC'S attention to their need, and Sudan played a large part in achieving that recognition. As early as 1974, the Rabat Arab summit meeting had selected Khartoum as the headquarters of BADEA. Algeria had initially sought to host the Bank, but "realizing that Khartoum was the best headquarters for the Bank because of Sudan's position in Africa",[23] Algerian President Houari Boumedienne yielded. The

---

21. Sudanow, Vol. III, No. 2, February 1978, p. 27-28.
22. Al-Sahafa, Khartoum, 22 January 1974, p.2.
23. Al-Ayam, Khartoum, 31 October 1974, p. 1.

Sudan immediately subscribed a million dollars to BADEA a limited amount when compared with the share paid by Saudi Arabia or Kuwait, but a generous one in view of the country's dire economic situation. Sudan's limited capacity to contribute financially to the institutions of Afro-Arab cooperation was the only serious limitation of its role. Nevertheless, Sudan contributed positively to Afro-Arab cooperation, perhaps most usefully by providing a model of Arabs and Blacks living harmoniously in the years after the Addis Ababa Agreement.

Benefits to Sudan

Sudan benefited from Afro-Arab cooperation economically, politically, and socially. Economically, the regime utilized Sudan's special position in Afro-Arab cooperation to focus the attention of the Arab countries on her own potential. The Nimeiri government appealed to the Arab countries to strengthen Sudan so it could act as the Arabs extension in Black Africa. The response was positive and Arab aid to Sudan increased from $33 million in 1972 to $220 million in 1974. Saudi Arabia guaranteed a Euro-dollar loan of $200 million for the Sudan in 1974, while the Saudi Arabian Monetary Agency loaned $150 million to meet immediate budgetary needs at the beginning of 1974.[24]

Arab capital was instrumental in such key projects as the Rahad and Kenana sugar schemes and the Khartoum-Port Sudan road. The Rahad scheme is capitalized at $400 million, of which the Kuwait Fund for Arab Economic Development paid $50 million and the Saudi Development Fund another $28 million. The Kuwaiti and Saudi

24. "Sudan Special", in New African, January 1978, No. 125, p.48.

shares represented about half of the foreign currency invested in the project.[25] Similarly, most of the $500 million capital of the Kenana sugar project came from Saudi Arabia and Kuwait. Another agreement, signed July 1977, provided $99 million from the Saudi Development Fund for the improvement of Sudan's railways, the establishment of fourteen earth satellite stations, and the purchase of new equipment for civil aviation. The Kuwait Fund for Arab Economic Development contributed $17.4 million to the railways, with the Abu Dhabi Fund for Arab Economic Development adding $10 million more. Kuwait also started a joint venture with the Sudanese government to construct two huge poultry complexes south of Khartoum. The project produces 50 million eggs and 30 million chickens annually.[26]

In 1976 twelve Arab governments established in Khartoum the Arab authority for Agricultural Investment and Development (AAAID), with a capital of $510 million. It planned to invest only in Sudan, expecting to finance sixty-one agricultural projects in various parts of the country over the following twenty-five years at a total cost of $220 million. Three years later, the Emirates-Sudan Investment Company set up three subsidiary companies: the Emirates-Khartoum Investment Company, the Emirates-Gezira Investment Company, and the Emirates-Red Sea Investment Company. The Emirates-Khartoum Company and the Emirates-Red Sea Company each had a capital of Ls.7.5 million of which the Emirates-Sudan Company provided two-third. The Emirates-Gezira Company had a capital of Ls.3.75 million provided by the mother company and Gezira province on a similar two-to-one

---

25. Ibid, p.63.

26. "Sudan Special", p.63

basis. The activities of the companies included building hotels, poultry and livestock farms, and agricultural investment.[27]

All these examples reveal how Sudan, more than any other Arab or African country, has succeeded in utilizing Afro-Arab cooperation for its own benefit. Besides the economic gains there have also been political gains. By stressing that it was the country most suited - racially and geographically - to link Arabs and Africans, Sudan sought an active regional role and international prestige. Sudan also benefited racially from Afro-Arab cooperation in that an important goal of the May Regime was to prevent the emergence of racial tension between Arabs and non-Arabs in Sudan. The solidarity and cooperation between the Arab and the Black African countries was reflected in national unity inside Sudan. Had the Arab countries and the Black African states continued to mistrust each other, as had been the case during the 1960s, Sudan would probably have been forced to take sides. In such a situation the Arab Sudanese would most probably have sided with the Arab countries, while the non-Arab Sudanese would have sided with the Black African countries, thereby assuring internal friction. But, with Afro-Arab cooperation, this prospect was minimized. Sudan, then, played an active role in Afro-Arab cooperation, successfully utilizing its racial and geographical position and, in return, benefiting more than any other country from Afro-Arab cooperation.

---

27. Sudanow, Vol. IV, No. 2, February 1979, p. 41.

AN INVENTORY OF FOREIGN AID TO THE SUDAN

By
Abdel Basit Saeed

Sizeable amounts of foreign capital entered the Sudan prior to independence in 1956, primarily from Great Britain and Egypt, the partners in the condominium government. The capital inflow from the condominium powers between the two world wars and afterwards until independence made it possible for the Sudan to implement such major development projects as the single track railway to Port Sudan, and the well known Gezira scheme. In economic terms these projects constituted a great material heritage, which the Sudan continued to develop as its economic infrastructure expanded after independence. Another important point about the capital which entered the country prior to independence was that "lenders" considered it a debt repayable by the Sudan government and so demanded repayment even after independence. Table 1 summarizes the state of loans and repayments in 1956.

Data on Sudan's debts to the condominium powers has been very difficult to obtain. The investment projects which were financed by foreign resources prior to independence laid the foundation for the modern sector and helped augment domestic resources, thus making it possible to make subsequent investments and meet debt repayments from domestic savings. They also resulted in a rise in income which made it possible for the economy to meet most of its limited investment requirements during the early 1950s, especially in the years immediately preceeding independence. Schemes established as a result of this capital inflow contributed substantially

TABLE 1*
Foreign capital inflow before 1956 (in £E million)*

Grants and Loans	Original Amount Borrowed	Balance to be repaid by 1956
London Money Market Loans		
5½% guaranteed bonds	6,220,500	Repaid
4½% guaranteed stock	3,669,316	2,546,213
4% guaranteed stock	1,462,500	1,223,353
3½% guaranteed stock	1,950,000	564,818
4½% guaranteed stock	1,404,000	Repaid
5% guaranteed stock	2,106,000	779,243
21% guaranteed stock	526,500	Repaid
Egyptian loans	5,414,525	4,363,525
Egyptian grants	2,800,000	
British grants	99,500	

* Ali Abdalla Ali, "The Flow and Use of Foreign Funds in the Democratic Republic of the Sudan 1969-1971 - Discussion Paper," Social and Economic Research Council, Khartoum, Bulletin No. 15, 19 January 1975.

** The Egyptian pound was the only official currency in circulation in the Sudan prior to 1956.

to the execution and success of other development programmes in the period 1941-1951 and 1951-1955, which were mainly directed towards building infrastructure and providing social services.

Table 1 shows that the total foreign capital inflow (loans and grants) extended by the condominium powers up to 1956 reached £E 25.85 million. 11.5% of the total inflow (£E 2.9 million) was extended as grants and the remaining 88.5% (£E 22.95 million) as loans. The guaranteed element of bonds and stocks issued on the London money market ranged between 3½% and a record high of 21%. This table also shows that grants constituted only 13% of the total funds involved. Out of Sudan's total outstanding debt at independence only £E 9.48 was repayable by 1956.

Table 2 shows that the maturity of each loan extends to 40 years, while the price varied between 4% and 5%. Total proceeds reached S£ 10.12 million and went to agriculture, irrigation, and transportation. It will be shown later that most British aid after independence went to the same economic sectors.

Table 1 and 2 are difficult to compare, first because the former uses the Egyptian pound as its unit of account while the latter uses the Sudanese pound. Secondly, the tables cover different time scales. In any event, suffice it to mention that the tradition of borrowing was already established in the Sudan by the time it became independent and that its indebtedness approximated £E25 million in 1956. The point is that these £E25 million were considered an outstanding debt even though they do not qualify as aid.

TABLE 2
Sudan government guaranteed loans on 31 December 1924*

date of issue	maturity	price	net proceeds in £S
October 1919	1929-59	5½% guaranteed bonds 95½%	3,342,500
February 1921	1929-59	5½% guaranteed bonds 92 %	2,649,600
January 1923	1939-73	4½% guaranteed stock 93 %	3,022,500
May 1924	1939-73	4% guaranteed stock 95¼%	489,120
November 1924	1950-74	4% guaranteed stock 86 %	645,000

* Abdel Rahman Abdel Wahab, "Development Planning in the Sudan: Policy and Organization", in Ali Mohamed El Hasan (ed.), An Introduction to the Sudan Economy, (Khartoum University Press, 1976).

Railway extension	700,000
Loan to Sudan plantation syndicate	400,000
Sennar dam and canalization	8,702,754
Cost of issue	261,027
Balance unspent	84,831

FOREIGN AID AFTER 1956

The figures in Table 3 show that the Sudan is an aid-dependent country as opposed to those developing countries which borrow from private banks to finance particular projects. TAble 4 shows that official foreign loans between 1956 and 1976 approximated £S538 million, making an average annual borrowing rate from multilateral and bilateral sources of £S26.5 million. Borrowing from such multilateral sources as the World Bank and the African Development Bank (ADB) reached about £S127 million or 23.6% of the total of official loans. However, the World Bank alone provided 21 loans for various projects in different sectors totalling £S119.3 million, or 22.2% of the foreign loans, or 1.4% of the total volume.

The table also shows that bilateral capital aid from the three main sources amounted to £S411.3 million or 75.4% of the total. The Arab states and Arab financial institutions were in the forefront, contributing some £S175 million between these two decades. Arab official capital aid was 32.5% of the total official loans. The £S175 million represented 42.6% of the total of official bilateral loans. Next came bilateral aid from Western European countries, the United States of America and Japan. These free market economies extended £S141 million or 26.2% of the total official aid commitments to Sudan between 1956 and 1976. This was 34% of the total bilateral aid.

The third group of bilateral donors consists of countries with centrally planned economies, such as the Soviet Union, China, and the socialist states of Eastern Europe. This group extended loans amounting to £S95.3 million or only 17.7% of the total loans extended

TABLE 3

Statistical summary of types and volume of foreign aid to the Sudan, 1956 to 1976 (£S million)*

type of aid	amount	type of aid as % of total
loans	537,97	70.5%
grants	55,82	7.3%
credit facilities	119.71	15.7%
technical and food aid	49.60	6.5%
todal	763.1	100.%

* Ministry of National Planning, "The Situation of Foreign Loans and Credit Facilities Obtained by the Sudan". (Unpublished report submitted to Council of Ministers, Ministry of National Planning, Khartoum, August 1977), p.4. (Translated from Arabic).

TABLE 4
Statistical summary of volume by source of foreign capital inflow to the sudan between 1956 and 1976* (in £S million)

source of aid	volume of capital commitments	% of total	with-drawn	% utilization **
IBRD group	119.3	22.2	77.12	64.64
Arab states and Arab financial institutions	174.9	32.5	83.4	47.68
Western Europe, USA, and Japan	141.07	26.2	82.7	58.6
East European socialist countries, USSR, China and North Korea	95.3	17.7	46.64	48.94
African Development Bank	7.4	1.4	3.1	41.89

* Ibid., p.5. Statistics in this Table summarize gross capital aid commitments as of December 1976.

** Percentage utilization refers to the ratio of withdrawals as a percentage of the total volume of capital aid commitments made by the corresponding group of donors.

to the Sudan in the years 1956-1976. Socialist aid commitments were 23.1% of total bilateral aid during the period.

A point to be made here is that the Sudan depended heavily on bilateral and multilateral aid to supplement its poor domestic resources with a view to facilitating and executing its development efforts. However, the statistics reveal that the total amount of foreign loans actually received was £S292.96 million, or 54.5% of the official capital aid commitments.

Table 5 shows the sectoral distribution of bilateral and multilateral loans obtained between 1958 and 1976. Of the £S538 million noted on Table 4, 32.5% (£S174.8 million) went to the transport and communications sector. About 12% of the commitments to this sector were made prior to the inauguration of the Ten Year Plan, while another 12% were made during the first five years of the Ten Year Plan. The years 1966-1969 witnessed negligible aid commitments to the transport and communications sector, but these increased significantly between 1970 and 1976. Figures show that there were three peaks: £S17.6 million in 1970, £S18 million in 1974, and £S80.0 million in 1976. About 76% of capital aid commitments to this sector (£S312 million) have been made during the regime of General Nimeiri. This is the period starting with the Russian engineered Five Year Plan, which was revised after the abortive coup attempt of July 1971 and labled the Phased Programme of National Action. This programme, as shall be illustrated later, marked the beginning of significant change in the orientation of domestic economic policy from the East European socialist countries to the Western European countries and Arab states.

TABLE 5
Sectoral distribution of loans, 1958-1976 (in £S million)*

years	transportation & communications	agriculture	industry	services	capital goods		
'58	13.6						
'59	7.8						
'60		5.4	3.9				
'61	2.7	21.1	8.0				
'62	7.1		2.6				
'63			2.5		7.1		
'64							
'65	10.8		5.2		3.2		
'66		1.4					
'67		4.9					
'68		4.8		9.5			
'69	0.3	5.4		2.0	6.2		
'70	17.6	1.0		1.3			
'71	2.1	31.3					
'72	2.8	5.8			32.7		
'73		44.2	14.1		8.2		
'74	18.0	4.8	8.3	3.0	11.1		
'75	11.2	23.3	16.8	11.5	14.8		
''76	80.0	13.2	12.6	4.5	6.7		
sub-total	174.8	166.6	74.0	31.8	90.8	total loans	538.0
sub-total % of total**	32.5%	31.0%	13.7%	5.9%	16.9%	total percentage	100%

* calculated from data provided by the Ministry of National Planning, Khartoum, June, 1977.

** In calculating this percentage, figures in the sub-total column were rounded to the nearest whole £S million before making the calculations.

Commitments to the agricultural sector (including irrigation and livestock), reached about £S165 million, or 31% of the total commitment. No significant commitments were made to this sector before the inauguration of the Ten Year Plan. In the fiscal year 1960-1961 - the first year of the Ten Year Plan - £S26.5 million (15.8% of all commitments that would be made in this area) entered the agricultural sector. No further commitments were made to this sector between 1962 and 1965.

The industrial sector started to receive aid with the inauguration of the Ten Year Plan. Loans of £S74 million were granted to this sector from 1956 to 1976 but this amounted to only 13.7% of all loans. Roughly one-third of these credits (£S22.2 million) date from 1960-1965. After a seven year gap, loans to promote industry resumed and had amounted to 51.8 million by the end of the period.

Loans for the service sector, all of which were made after 1967, totalled £S31.8 million, and constituted 5.9% of all loans. Three loans which amounted to £S12.8 million were made between 1968 and 1970. There were no loans from 1971 to 1973, but £S19 million of loan capital was promised to this sector between 1974 and 1976. Of the £S31.8 million promised for services from 1958 to 1976, only £S9.5 million were obtained before 1969.

A fifth purpose for which sizeable amounts of capital were borrowed was the purchase of industrial capital and quasi-capital goods. Loans towards this end amounted to £S90.8 million (16.9% of all loans secured between 1958 and 1976). None of these loans was made before 1963. 18.2% of the loans to this sector (£S16.5 million) date from 1963-1969. From 1972 to 1976 there was a continuous flow of loans for the purchase of capital goods.

81.8% of the loans to this sector came between 1972 and 1976.

Table 5 reveals an insignificant inflow of foreign aid in the pre-plan period (1956-1960). Some capital was attracted in the opening few years of the Ten Year Plan (1960-1963), but it was little in comparison to amounts offered after 1969. However, between 1956 and 1964, (during the first two republics) the Sudan received 24% of the loans which would fall to the transport sector, 15.8% of those destined for agriculture, 30% of the capital which would benefit the industrial sector, and none of those which would eventually flow to the services sector. From 1956 to 1969 the Sudanese obtained 9.9% of the total extended to the agricultural sector, virtually nothing for the industrial sector, and about 37% of the capital designed to assist services.

Since the May Revolution of 1969, several policies to attract foreign loans have been tried. Between 1969 and 1976, the Sudan obtained 76% of all loans made to the transport and communications sector, 74.3% of those intended for the agricultural sector, 70% of those for the industrial sector, 59.4% of those aimed at the services sector and 81.8% of those to be used for the purchase of industrial capital goods.

CREDIT FACILITIES

Sudan's experience with commercial credit facilities and commercial borrowing began in 1966. From 1966-1968, two credit facilities amounting to £S2.8 million were made available to the Sudan by Western European sources. In 1969 and 1970 both Western and Eastern European sources extended more credit facilities. Capital inflow from credit facilities in this period amounted to £S116.5 million. Credit facilities made available by the socialist countries (Yugoslavia and East Germany) in 1969 and 1970 amounted to £S12.5 million or 10.5% of the total value of credit facilities obtained between 1966 and 1976. Credit facilities extended by socialist countries bore an annual interest rate of between 7% and 8% and capital acquired through them was repayable in seven and ten years. Credit facilities from the socialist countries were used to purchase equipment for drilling artesian wells and for the Port Sudan weaving factory, as well as for building a regional assembly complex at Juba.

Credit facilities extended by Western European countries and finance institutions amounted to £S106.8 million or 89.5% of Sudan's total credit facilities between 1966 and 1976. The terms and conditions under which such credit was extended were generally more stringent than those of loans. The average interest rate for Western European credit facilities was 7% while the redemption period varied between five and twelve years. Those credit facilities extended at less than 3% interest usually included market "LIBOR" (London Interbank Offering Rate). Such loans are customarily floating-rate notes priced by charging the borrower the cost of Euro-currency funds to the lending financial institutions, banks or companies or, in other words, by charging the LIBOR at the beginning of each payment period plus an additional percentage known as the "spread over LIBOR".

Statistics show the sectoral distribution of credit facilities as follows: £S86.7 million (72.5%) to the industrial sector ;£S13.6 million (11.6%) to the transport and communications sector ;£S8.65 million (7.5%) to the service sector ;and £S3.8 million (3.3%) not allocated to any particular sector.

TABLE 6

Statistical summary of the volume of technical assistance and food aid extended by the United Nations system and bilateral donors*

source of assistance	value in £S million
United Nations system:	
World Food Programme	18.3
U.N.D.P.	17.8
Bilateral technical cooperation:	
United Kingdom	2.5
Netherlands	3.5
West Germany	6.6
Sweden	0.8

* Ministry of National Planning, "The Situation of Foreign Loans and Credit Facilities Obtained by the Sudan", (Report prepared by the Ministry of National Planning, Khartoum, August 1977. p.6. (Translated from Arabic).

Table 7
Educational assistance extended to Sudan at the undergraduate level, 1973-1977*

donor	approx. amount in £S m	73–74	74–75	75–76	76–77	77–78	total
Egypt	22.9	363	671	1027	1279	2296	5736
USSR	10.7	74	7	152	–	–	233
Romania	11.0	73	53	35	40	113	314
Yugoslavia	0.2	14	6	6	5	7	38
Czechoslovakia	0.1	9	3	5	5	5	27
Saudi Arabia	0.3	12	20	23	10	10	75
West Germany	0.06	–	1	7	6	–	14
East Germany	0.1	16	7	–	5	–	28
Poland	0.05	–	2	5	5	–	12
Bulgaria	0.1	2	6	11	5	–	24
Kuwait	0.03	–	2	1	2	2	7
Hungary	0.25	16	14	12	10	10	62
China	0.14	4	7	7	5	13	36
Morocco	0.23	–	9	32	–	20	61
Iraq	0.1	5	3	4	6	7	25
Pakistan	0.04	–	1	–	4	5	10
India	0.04	6	3	–	–	2	9
Tanzania	0.04	–	–	11	–	2	11
Kenya	0.01	–	–	2	–	–	2
Greece	0.01	–	6	–	–	–	6
Switzerland	0.01	–	3	–	–	–	3
Iran	0.01	–	3	–	–	–	3
Algeria	0.03	–	–	–	4	5	8
TOTAL	46.32	594	827	1340	1390	2495	6646

* Ministry of Education, Cultural Relations Dept., Dec. 1976.

TABLE 8
Projected, committed, and actual inflow of loan capital: 1957/1958 - 1974/1975*

years	projected loan capital	committed loan capital	actual loan capital
57-58	-		4.8
58-59	-	13.6	7.5
59-60	-	7.8	11.1
60-61	-	9.3	12.8
Line A	-	30.7	36.8
61-62	23.1	31.8	12.3
62-63	19.2	9.7	11.6
63-64	18.6	7.4	8.9
64-65	16.3	-	15.5
65-66	14.4	17.0	8.3
66-67	12.6	1.4	16.6
67-68	12.2	14.6	9.3
68-69	11.6	18.5	5.5
69-70	11.6	7.3	12.2
70-71	10.3	-	-
Line B	149.9	107.7	110.2
71-72	22.5	35.8	3.8
72-73	23.5	39.1	7.5
73-74	25.2	82.6	9.4
74-75	19.7	44.1	111.5
Line C	109.6	221.5	132.2
GRAND TOTAL	259.5	359.9	279.2

* Data in this table has been compiled from tables available in TYP and FYP official documents, several economic surveys, and tables on foreign aid commitments covering the years since 1958 provided by the Planning Commission in October 1976 and early May. 1977.

TABLE 9

SOURCE	'58	'59	'60	'61	'62	'63	'64	'65	'66
IBRD	13.6		5.4	11.3				10.8	
Kuwait					6.8			1.7	
Saudi Arabia									
Arab Emirates									
Egypt									
AFED									
United Arab Bank									
West Germany			3.9	6.4	1.9				
Netherlands					0.3			1.0	
Britain		4.9		2.7		4.9			
Sweden									1.4
Italy				3.4					
Denmark									
USA					.7	2.5			
Japan									
France									
Bulgium									
ADB									
Yugoslavia		7.8							
Czechoslovakia								3.5	
USSR				8.0					
Bulgaria									
East Germany									
Hungary									
Rumania									
China									
N. Korea									
Libya									
Algeria									

'67	'68	'69	'70	'71	'72	'73	'74	'75	'76	TOTAL
	11.4				6.3	16	12.1	13.9	11.5	112.3
4.9				16.2	1.6	29.9		14.4	11.9	87.4
								9.7	12.8	22.5
				3.5					19.6	23.1
.7	7.1									7.8
							9.6	8.8	13.2	31.6
									2.5	2.5
					5.5	6.0	8.9	11.1	22.0	65.5
								1.5	1.7	4.5
		.6			0.3	8.6				30.3
			1.0							2.4
5.0		.07			0.4	1.5		5.5		15.9
				.7			1.1			1.8
						13.6			4.2	21.0
									3.4	3.4
									6.2	6.2
									1.8	1.8
				1.3			4.1		2.0	7.4
										7.8
						7.0				10.5
	2.0									10.0
5.0										5.0
	4.0									4.0
		3.5								3.5
					25.0					25.0
		14.1	14.1							28.2
		1.3								1.3
	6.05									6.05
.7										.7

Educational aid is one type of technical assistance from which the Sudan stands to benefit from the resourses of other countries. It should be noted that Western European countries do not extend educational assistance at the undergraduate level. The socialist countries of Eastern Europe and some Arab countries such as Kuwait, Saudi Arabia and Iraq have extended such educational assistance.

Egypt dominated the field of educational assistance to the Sudan in the period under study, supporting university education for 5736 students. The cost of educating this number of students for four years was the equivalent of £S23 million; the USSR spent £S10.7 million; and Romania another £S6.11 million. These three countries accounted for 97.7% of all educational assistance extended to the Sudan between 1973 and 1977. The magnitude of educational assistance rose every year after 1974, from £S594 in that year to £S2495 in 1977-1978. This increase is consonant with the general rise in foreign capital aid in the same period, as shown earlier.

Table 8 indicates three periods of foreign capital inflow. Line A shows that there were no projections for the years 1957 to 1961. It also shows that foreign donors made commitments amounting to £S30.7 million. The foreign capital which the Sudan actually received during these years, however, was £S36.8 million.

Several facts must be borne in mind to understand these figures. First, there was no set development plan with identificable objectives to guide the country's development efforts in the first two years of independence or the first two years of the military regime which General Ibrahim Abboud headed beginning in November 1958. It was that government which instituted the first comprehensive attempt at economic planning in the form of the Ten Year Plan. What had existed from 1956 to 1961 was the so-called "New Scheme Programmes, launched in 1957, lumped together 273 unconnected projects. In the early years of independence, however, constitutional and administrative reform took precedence over economic policy, and little emphasis was given to the recruitment of foreign capital.

Soon there were some foreign capital commitments in this period, one must conclude that the Sudan did request some external financing. The fact that aid extended at this early state came from the IBRD, West Germany, and Yugoslavia[1] - the first two of which do not usually extend aid unless it is officially requested, supports this conclusion. In the absence of specifically showing the sources of disbursements, however, the conclusion remains speculative.

The second period of capital inflow coincides with the Ten Year Plan. Line B shows projections of nearly £S150 million. While foreign donors' commitments reached 72% of the projections, the actual amount received fell some 27% short of expectations.

Line C deals with projections, commitments and disbursements during the Five Year Plan. Its Soviet architects estimated the foreign capital requirements at about £S95 million. In 1970 the Sudan obtained from the Socialist bloc almost all the necessary outside funds to meet 47% of the estimated costs of the Five Year Plan. However, disbursements of funds promised by these countries when the plan was set up had reached

1. From a table on foreign aid sources provided by the Economic Research Section, Ministry of Finance, Planning, and National Economy, May 1977.

only 51% of commitments by 1975. With the rupture in political relations and the halting of socialist aid after the July 1971 coup attempt the Sudan had to revise the Five Year plan and look elsewhere - to Western capitalist countries - for foreign aid. Commitments leaped from £S20 million in 1970/71 to £S39 million in 1972/73 and to £S83 million in 1973/74. The new donors whom Sudan approached after the coup attempt enthusiastically promised large amounts of foreign capital. This is borne out by the 200% growth from the plan's projections (£S 110 million) and commitments (£S221.5 million). Lines A and B reveal that actual capital inflow in the pre-plan period (1957-1960) and in Ten Year Plan period (1961-1971) exceeded donors' commitments. This did not occur during the Five Year Plan, largely because of the drastic change in orientation from the Eastern Bloc to the Western countries. In the eighteen years covered by the table, the total foreign capital actually received (£S274 million) exceeded Sudan's original projections of £S260 million by about 15%, whereas it fell short of the donors' commitments of £S360 million by some £S86 million.

The two development plans and the "New Schemes programme" which preceeded them, always included a foreign capital component to facilitate the realization of their objectives. This foreign capital component was 25.4% of the total investment of the Ten Year Plan and 47% of the Five Year Plan. Clearly, then, it has been the duty and the vested interest of every government in the Sudan since independence - regardless of its political slogans or ideological overtones to acquire foreign aid for development purposes. Therefore, one may conclude that between 1956 and 1976 the recruitment of foreign capital has been a primary national interest of the Sudan, and as such, a major factor in foreign policy decisions. It could also be argued that the failure of the Ten Year Plan and the Five Year Plan to achieve their projections fully suggests that aid oriented development plans have either failed to stimulate expected activity or have produced growth without development.

According to Table 9, multinational donors such as the World Bank Group, the Arab Fund for Economic and Social Development, and the African Development Bank extended 27.2% of the aid commitments. The Arab Fund and the African Development Bank came forward with aid only after 1971, while IBRD began extending aid in 1958. Multinational aid extended to the Sudan (£S151.3 million) made up 37% of all bilateral aid, with IBRD and its soft loan agency IDA heading the list of donors.

Western capitalist countries, multilateral donors, and Arab donors contributed almost equally to Sudan's development from 1956 to 1976. The Arabs contributed 27.2% of the aid; and Western European countries, the U.S.A., and Japan donated another 27.7%. The Communist Bloc came last, with commitments from the Eastern European socialist countries and China representing only 17.3%. Thus, the Sudan's foreign aid experience did not reflect domination of, or dependence on, any particular group of countries. Neither the capitalist camp nor the communist bloc was in a position to manipulate foreign capital inflow. Neither the U.S.A. nor the USSR dominated the aid picture, although American contributions were concentrated in two different periods. The initial aid came during the first military regime, but it slowed down in 1964, and ceased altogether in 1967 when the Sudan severed relations as a result of the June War. American aid was again made available in 1973, after political development made Sudan a "friend" of the Western countries.

To elaborate on this theme further, Table 9 may be viewed from a different angle - in terms of whether the funds came Western capitalists, Arab, or Communist sources. In this analysis, multilateral and bilateral sources will be excluded as such, although both the World Bank and IBRD, owing to the sources of their funds, will be treated as western contributors. The table shows that of the multinational donations, £S112.3 million is World Bank money while £S39 million originated with the Arab Fund for Economic and Social Development and the Afican Development Bank. Capital aid commitments from other Western sources totalled £S152.8 million, bringing "western money" to approximately £S265 million, or 48.2% of the total. "Arab money" represented a third of all commitments, while Communist contributions of £S95 million comprised a 17.2% share. China and Romania alone accounted for £S53.2 million (56%) of the Communist commitments. Since these two commitments came in 1970 and 1971, it is obvious that the contribution of Eastern European countries before 1970 was very low. "Western money" predominated over other sources, followed by "Arab money", and then "Communist money". This overview of capital aid commitments does not contradict the points made in the previous categorization of individual donors. Rather, it indicates that the Sudan depended largely on Western capital without being dominated by any particular donor.

TABLE 10
The sequence of donors

donors	1958 - 1976 commitments*	commitments as % of the total**
IBRD Group	112.0	20.0%
Kuwait	87.0	15.8%
West Germany	66.0	12.0%
AFSED	32.0	5.8%
Britain	30.0	5.5%
China	28.0	5.0%
Romania	25.0	4.5%
United Arab Emirates	23.0	4.2%
Saudi Arabia	23.0	4.2%
U.S.A.	21.0	3.5%
Italy	16.0	2.9%
Czechoslovakia	11.0	2.0%
USSR	10.0	1.8%
African Development Bank and African Development Fund	8.0	1.4%

* Approximated in £.S. million to the nearest whole million.

** About 11.6% of the total commitments were made by such minor donors as Egypt, the United Arab Bank, Denmark, Yugoslavia, Bulgaria, North Korea, Libya, Algeria, and Sweden. This 11.6% brings the total to 100%.

TABLE 11
Volume of capital aid and credit facilities commitments and disbursements received by Different regimes (in £S million)*

source	58-64	65-69	70-76	TOTAL
IBRD Group				
commitments	30.3	22.2	73.2	119.3
disbursements	30.3	20.6	29.4	80.3
Western Europe and USA				
commitments	26.7	7.5	111.8	146.0
disbursements	28.8	7.0	16.7	97.5
Socialist countries & China				
commitments	17.8	12.5	65.0	95.3
disbursements	14.0	9.2	24.0	47.2
Arab countries & Arab finance institutions				
commitments	6.8	14.4	153.7	174.9
disbursements	6.8	14.4	67.5	88.7
Total Commitments	81.6	65.6	505.0	
Total Disbursements	80.0	51.2	182.6	

* Calculated from figures in Table 9 above and from tables provided by the Ministry of National Planning, Khartoum, May 1977.

From Table 9 may be extrapolated Table 10, a sequence of major, medium, and minor donors.[2] The U.S.A. and the USSR, the two great powers, rank tenth and thirteenth respectively. Multilateral donors top the list, followed by Kuwait and West Germany.

Table 11 is a corollary of Table 9 in that it deals with governments while the other deals with particular years. During the first military regime, capital aid commitments reached £S82 million, about 12% of the total amount. Actual capital inflow in this period (1958-64) was some £S80 million, or 25% of all actual disbursements. Capital aid commitments in the 1965-69 regime were about £S66 million or 10.2% of the total, while disbursements fell short of commitments by about £S15 million. Actual foreign capital inflow in this period equalled 16.6% of the total obtained by the Sudan from 1956 to 1976. The period 1970-76 saw very large amounts of capital aid commitments and disbursements. 77.8% of all commitments extended to the Sudan between independence and 1976 stemmed from the efforts of the present government to obtain foreign aid. Inflow was quite substantial in comparison with earlier disbursements. Approximately 58% of the total capital inflow dated from these years.

During the first two regimes, the World Bank and other multilateral doners dominated Sudan's foreign aid. The Arab countries dominated in the 1970-76 period, followed by Western European donors, the multilateral donors, and, finally, the Socialist countries.

---

2. Commitments between £S 1-19 million are minor, £S 20-29 million medium, and over £S 30 million major.

Aid from West Germany

The influence of German aid on the development policies of recipient countries, especially in Africa, has been small, perhaps because Germany only became a full fledged member of the "donor club" relatively recently. Germany started transfering capital to the Sudan in 1960. Moreover, Germany, unlike Britain and France, had few traditional spheres of influence in which it could naturally concentrate. It follows that no single aid recipient has been wholly or inextricably dependent on German aid for any length of time. An unintended consequence of this situation was that little attention was paid to Germany before the late 1960s in less developed countries, especially in Africa. Largely for these reasons, Germany adopted a "banking approach" to aid in which it looks at each project in isolation, considering its merits and demerits, and gives aid only if the project satisfies certain economic, commercial, and managerial criteria. An important criterion has been that the recipient country must share in the responsibility - political, administrative, and financial - for German aid projects. A local contribution to the project, however small, is insisted upon. In the Sudan, especially after 1972, the Germans showed considerable leniency in the aid terms offered. The local currency component has been limited to the provision of minimal services such as unloading at Port Sudan and carried by German flag vessels. The German preference is for projects that have been studied and carefully planned, and merely await financing so that the lengthy procedure required by the "Kreditanstalt fur Wiederaufbau" (KFW) would be cut to a minimum. The absence of planned and economically viable projects in

1972 and 1973 when Sudan requested German aid negatively affected the amount extended to the Sudan. The German authorities also tend to be critical of requests involving luxury items for recipient countries. For example, in 1973 they refused to grant a loan requested by the Sudanese Ministry of Interior for the purchase of Mercedes Benz saloons.[3] Similarly, more favorable consideration is accorded to countries which adopt policies to combat and control inflation, encourage processes that may lead to the accumulation of local national capital for investment, reform their tax systems, and attempt to keep the import of luxury items to a minimum.

The KFW grants and administers capital aid loans on behalf of the Federal government on the basis of criteria established in cooperation with the Bonn government but with variations according to the principles cited above. The four major steps to securing German aid begin when the borrower makes an application and presents all supporting data for assessing the application to the Federal government. Then the KFW appraises the project's economic and technical soundness and its worthiness from a macro-economic viewpoint as well as from the aspect of social and economic development, after which the Federal government uses these reports and recommendations to determine the eligibility of the project for German money. Thirdly, if the Federal government decrees the project worthy of promotion it charges the KFW with negotiation of the loan agreement, which specifies the terms and conditions under which the aid is being granted. Finally, the borrower ratifies the

---

3. Ministry of Foreign Affairs, Khartoum, File No. 9, p.20.

agreement and places purchase orders. KFW disburses the loan, supervises debt servicing, and assesses the success of the project after it is operational.[4]

Sudanese-German Aid and Trade Relations

Sudan's relations with West Germany strengthened in the early 1960s. Germany extended its loan, amounting to £S4 million on the inauguration of the Ten Year Plan. Additional loans of £S6.4 million in 1961 and £S1.93 million in 1962 accrued to the irrigation and agricultural sectors. Of these £S 12.33 million, 5.93 million went to the Gineid and Khashm el Girba sugar factories, with the remaining 6.4 million going to Roseiris dam - the largest project in the Ten Year Plan. In February 1963, an agreement encouraging German investment in the Sudan was signed, but for ten years after the 1962 grant there were no loans.

In February 1964, the Sudan raised the issue of foreign Christian missionaries' involvement in instigating the revolt in the south and acting as agents of "...colonialist imperialist conspiracies against the unity and integrity of the country ..."[5] The subsequent repatriation of foreign missionaries from the southern provinces soured relations with several European states. Contacts deteriorated further when Sudan

---

4. These four points have been assembled from documents on the actual negotiation of a German aid agreement in 1975. The author participated in those negotiations and in the distribution of the funds.

5. A nationwide declaration broadcast by the Sudanese Ministry of the Interior on 27 February 1964. The Declaration is entitled "Repatriation of Foreign Missionaries from the Southern Provinces". Its Ministry of the Interior number is M1/46/A/1.

severed diplomatic relations with Germany as a result of the 1967 June war. A third incident adversely affecting German-Sudanese relations was the recognition of the German Democratic Republic (GDR) in 1970 by the radical army officers responsible for the 1969 military coup.

The first of these incidents reveals how an internal political problem in the south affected Sudan's foreign relations and how a domestic issue escalated to the scale of an inter-state problem. It also emphasizes that the problem of the southern Sudan has been an important variable in Sudanese domestic and foreign policies. The second incident indicates how regional politics, and particularly the Middle East problem, could affect Sudan's relations with other countries, especially those Western European countries from which it received the largest amounts of aid and foreign investment.

Sudan's relations with West Germany regained momentum after the failure of the July 1971 coup attempt. In March 1972 the two countries initiated a "skeleton agreement ... regarding technical co-operation" which the President of the Sudan ratified as "The Sudan-Federal Republic of Germany Technical Co-operation Agreement (Ratification), Order No. 87, 1972". The accord took effect on 17 August, 1972 and has since been the basic document in Sudanese-German aid and economic and technical cooperation. Under article (2) of this agreement, the countries need not sign "total" agreements every time the Sudan requires economic aid or technical assistance, but "... may conclude agreements regarding individual projects of technical cooperation". Since 1972 German loans to the Sudan have been referred to in serial-number from - the first German loan, 1972

(£S5.5 million); the second German loan, 1973 (£S6 million); third German loan, 1974 (£S8.9 million); fourth German loan, 1975 (£S11.1 million); and fifth German loan, 1975 (£S22 million).[6]

After the ratification of the skeleton agreement, several agreements were signed for projects in the areas of training, carrying out feasibility studies for some projects, and dispatching experts and teachers to assist Sudan's development efforts. In this way German capital aid covers loans for particular projects as well as such related costs as equipment and the personnel required to install and operate it until the Sudan trains its own specialists under the terms of the skeleton agreement. Technical assistance is usually in the form of grants, while capital aid comes almost exclusively as loans.

Germany has also extended food aid to the Sudan under separate agreements reflecting the spirit of those concluded for capital aid. The first such aid came only one month after the ratification of the skeleton agreement and provided for 13,000 metric tons of bulk wheat, free of charge. Termed the 1971/72 aid agreement, this agreement was followed by another in fiscal year 1973/74 which amounted to 3.311 thousand metric tons.

Table 12 presents a statistical overview of West German aid. The loans of 1960 and 1962 went to the promotion of the sugar industry in two schemes at Guneid and Khashm el-Girba. They totalled £S5.93 million, or

---

6. Source: Ministry of National Planning. This sequence does not ignore the German loans prior to 1972. Starting the enumeration with loans extended after the resumption of relations in 1971 on the basis of the 1972 Skeleton Agreement was deemed more convenient.

TABLE 12
The volume and terms of capital aid commitments extended by West Germany, 1960-1976 (approximated to nearest £S million)*

effective date	amount	annual interest rate	maturity	repayment period	withdrawals	Benefiting Sector** A	IR	IN	TC	CG
1960	4	5%		4 yrs.	1961-64	4	X		X	
1961	6	4.75%	8 yrs.	20 yrs.	1969-81	6	X	X		
1962	2	6%	3 yrs.	13 yrs.	1965-73	2	X		X	
1972	6	2%	8 yrs.	50 yrs.	1980-2022	6				X
1973	6	.75%	10 yrs	50 yrs.	1983-2023	6				X
1974	9	.75%	10 yrs.	50 yrs.	1984-2024	9				X
1975	11	.75%	10 yrs.	50 yrs.	1985-2025	-				X
1976	22	.75%	10 yrs.	50 yrs.	1986-2026	-			X	X

* Ministry of national Planning, Khartoum, May 1976.

** A= Agriculture; IR= Irrigation; IN= Industry; TC= Transport and Communications; CG= Capital and Quasi capital goods.

47% of all German aid offered between 1960 and 1962. The remaining 53% was the 1961 loan of £S6.4 million for the construction of the Roseiris dam. Loans in this early period were generally smaller than those granted after the resumption of aid in 1972. They also bore higher interest rates, ranging between 4¾% and 6% per annum, and had a shorter grace period (from 3 to 8 years) than later loans (from 8 to 10 years). The most remarkable difference between the two groups of loans was in the redemption period. Four to twenty years at first, but fifty years for each of the later loans.

All German loans extended in the second phase were commodity loans for the purchase of German industrial capital and quasi-capital goods. Technical assistance and expertise with a portion of each loan earmarked for technical assistance has been an integral part of capital aid since 1972. An agreement on technical cooperation supplementing the skeleton agreement of August 1972, was signed in 1973 specifying areas in which German aid and expertise were required. The fields of transport and communications and agriculture were singled out and the Germans pledged to undertake feasibility studies for river transportation projects along the White Nile, the establishment of a power station in Khartoum North, the electrification of the Blue Nile Province, and pump irrigation schemes on the White Nile. In the area of technical assistance, Germany was to provide experts in the fields of administration and public services, forestry, veterinary science, and, for the Ministry of Foreign Affairs, telecommunications, but few experts were actually sent.

Table 13 shows the actual value of German technical assistance in the fiscal years 1972-73 and 1973-74. These statistics are drawn from a statement made by the

TABLE 13
German technical assistance 1972-1974

project	allocation in Dm.
Agricultural Research Station, Houdeiba	3,000,000
Vocational Training Center, Khartoum	6,000,000
Sudan Television	9,000,000
Training of Police Officers	460,000
Maintenance of Telex system, Ministry of the Interior	3,000,000
Anti-thirst campaign, delivery of four pumps	730,000
Lwatok tea factory, delivery of two generators	300,000
	22,490,000 *

(Furthermore, 40-50 scholarships were awarded annually for practical training).

* Dm 22,490,000 equals approximately £S2.8 million.

of payments problems and, last but not least, the unfortunate break in diplomatic relations.[8]

Table 14 shows a positive balance of trade for the Sudan during the decade 1965-1975. The balance of trade and German capital aid fluctuated as political relations between the two countries affected the trade pattern, as in the noticeable decline between 1968 and 1971, while diplomatic relations were broken. Germany supplied no foreign aid in those years, but the decline in trade transactions was slower than that of aid, which was abrupt. This suggests a close relationship in both the donor and the recipient country between political decision making and the extension of aid. The cessation of German aid in 1962 following the repatriation of Christian missionaries and the severence of diplomatic relations in 1967, each of which negatively affected Sudan's trade with Germany, as shown by the decline of the balance of trade from £S8 million in 1968 to only £S2 million in 1970. The slow rise in trade after 1972 was accompanied by an increase of some 300% in capital aid.

Italian Aid

Italy extends capital aid and technical assistance to other countries both directly and through the E.E.C. Normally, capital aid takes one of three forms: loans from the Italian government to the recipient government; or credit facilities extended and approved by the Italian private sector enterprises; or credit facilities extended and approved by the Italian government and administered by Italian export and import dealers. The

---

8. Translated from "Sudan Supplement" to the German economic magazine Handelsblatt, 24 November 1969. The information appears in Ministry of Foreign Affairs Khartoum, File No. 9 (Germany), March 1977.

German Embassy in Khartoum to the Sudanese Ministry of Foreign Affairs.[7] In comparing this £S3 million of technical aid with the total German capital inflow of £S12 million in the same two year period, it becomes clear that Germany extended at least 25% of its aid in the form of technical assistance and personnel.

An important feature of Sudan's economic relations with West Germany was that Sudan maintained a constantly positive balance of trade with Germany in the decade 1965-1975. (See Table 14). The minimum balance was £S1.2 million in 1966, while the maximum - £S7.6 million - occurred in 1968. The latter figure reflected purchases to which the two countries had committed themselves before the severence of diplomatic relations in 1967 which, not surprisingly, had a negative affect on German purchases from the Sudan. The 1968 record dropped to £S4.4 million in 1969, £S2.04 million in 1971. A gradual rise occurred with the restoration of diplomatic relations in 1972 and again in 1973.

A German economic publication, <u>Handelsblatt</u>, commented on the state of the balance of trade between the two countries in 1969.

> Economic relations between the Federal Republic and this trade-partner are marked by the fact that the Sudan has a considerable export surplus. According to German foreign trade statistics, in 1968 it reached high of Dm 123.3 million. The Federal Republic has, since 1968, been the most important importer of Sudanese cotton, followed by India and Italy. The fact that German exports last year were reduced by 10.7% is attributable to Sudan's balance

---

7. Ministry of Foreign Affairs, Khartoum, File No. 9 (<u>Germany</u>); Note of the German Embassy Khartoum, No.224/74 W1 455,00, 10 July, 1974.

TABLE 14
Sudan's balance of trade with West Germany 1956-1975 (approximated to one decimal) in £S million*

item	'65	'66	'67	'68	'69	'70	'71	'72	'73
exports	7.1	6.6	8.8	12.3	10.1	9.9	8.2	10.2	13.9
imports	3.9	5.2	4.2	4.6	5.8	7.8	6.7	7.1	9.9
balance of trade	+3.3	+1.2	+4.6	+7.6	+4.4	+2.0	+1.6	+3.1	+3.9

* Ministry of Foreign Affairs, Khartoum, File No.9 (Germany&, March 1977.

volume and frequency of Italian aid is generally affected by economic conditions in the recipient country; the volume of trade between Italy and the borrower; and Italian economic and political interests in and relations with the recipient country.[9]

Sudan's contacts with Italian aid started in 1961 when two credit facilities of £S3.4 million were extended to the public sector by the Italian agencies, "Torno" and "G.I.E. for use in the establishment of the Khashm el-Girba sugar project in connection with Sudan's Ten Year Plan. Italy granted a second loan, amounting to £S5 million, later, originating with "Bonifica", this loan went to the AbuNa'ama research station, the new Blue Nile Bridge, and Gedaref water supply. This relatively small amount came two years after the Sudan and Italy signed their first agreement on economic and technical cooperation in July 1965. In encouraging cooperation, the agreement stipulated that Italy would make available experts to train Sudanese personnel in various technical and scientific fields and to conduct feasibility studies for development projects in the Sudan. The Italians made it clear that since the Sudan tended to ask other countries to conduct feasibility studies for projects which those countries might finance, they would give priority in financing to projects whose feasibility studies had been conducted by Italian firms or government personnel.

In 1974 the two governments agreed to review the 1965 agreement so as to best serve Sudan's new interests as laid out in the Five Year Plan of 1970/71 - 1974/75 and the programme of national action adopted by the

---

9. Ministry of Foreign Affairs, Khartoum, File No. 9 (Italy).

Sudan government in 1974. New articles on economic, technical, scientific, and industrial co-operation were added.[10] The final text urged Italian public and private enterprises to invest in the Sudan under concessionary terms, with certain guarantees for the repatriation of profits and against confiscation and nationalisation. Table 15 shows that Italian official assistance in capital aid or credit facilities was less than £S15.5 million in the period 1961-1975. All Italian loans between 1961 and 1967 (£S7 million) went to the agricultural sector. All those between 1969 and 1975 went to the transport and communications sector, with the bulk of the money and expertise directed to the construction of highways and bridges. Thus, Italy divided its aid almost equally between the agricultural and the transport sectors.

Most Italian loans to the Sudan were extended as credit facilities whose interest rates were high in comparison with loans extended by West Germany. The interest rate of the 1967 loan was 4½%. Credit facilities approved by the Italian government and financed by such Italian private enterprises as Torno, G.I.E., and Bonifica from 1972 to 1975 were at higher rates of 9½%. In these cases the Italian government assumes 3½% of the interest, leaving 6% to be repaid by the Sudan government to the Italian enterprise which extended the credit facility. The grace periods of Italian loans and credit facilities are also slight in comparison with those of other donors. The grace period never exceeded three years for any loan extended between 1961 and 1975, while the redemption period ranged from three to eight years.

10. Ibid.

TABLE 15
The volume and terms of capital aid commitments extended by Italy 1961-1975 (£S million)*

effect-ive date	amount	annual inter-est rate	grace period	maturity	repay-ment period	with-draw-als	benefit-ing sector A	TC**
1961	2.5	5½%	2 yrs	11 yrs	1963-72	2.5	X	
1961	.89	5½%	2 yrs	11 yrs	1963-72	.89	X	
1967	4.0	4½%	2 yrs	13 yrs	1969-80	4.0	X	
1969	.07	6½%	3 yrs	11 yrs	1972-80	.07		X
1972	.44	6½%	2 yrs	10 yrs	1974-82	.4		X
1973	1.55	6½%	none	6 yrs	1974-79	1.5		X
1975	5.5	6½%	3 yrs	10 yrs	1978-85			X

* Ministry of National Planning, Khartoum, May 1977.

** A= Agriculture; TC= Transport and Communications.

Aid from Minor Western European Donors[11]

The previous two sections illustrate Sudan's experiences with a major donor (Germany) and a medium scale donor (Italy). Minor Western European donors are listed in Table 16 and include the Kingdom of the Netherlands (Holland), Sweden, Denmark, France, and Belgium. Japan has also been included in this group because of the capitalist form of its development.

None of these minor donors extended capital aid in excess of £S6 million, and their total contribution was only £S20 million, over a twenty year period. Holland accounted for 22% of the total (£S4.5 million) in four loans between 1962 and 1976; Sweden 12% (£S2.4 million) in two loans; and Denmark and Belgium 10%, each approximately £S1.9 million, in three loans. France contributed 31% of the total (£S6.2 million) with a single loan in 1976, while Japan contributed another 17% (£S3.4 million) in one loan. In view of their high GNPs, the contributions of these countries were negligible.

France and Belgium set the highest interest rate (7½%), the shortest grace period (3 years), and some of the shortest redemption periods of the minor donors. The harsh terms of these small, short term loans were most unsuitahle for Sudan's needs and economic conditions. Denmark and Sweden offered small amounts, but with substantial redemption periods and a low interest rate of 2% in the case of Sweden and no interest on the Danish loan. The specifics of the loans from the Netherlands are taken as a case study in the following pages because of the length of the Sudanese-Dutch relationship.

---

11. The term minor donor applies to any country extending to the Sudan capital aid not exceeding £S10 million between 1956 and 1976.

31% of the minor loans went to the industrial section; 27% to the transport and communications sector; 21% to agriculture and a similar percentage towards the purchase of industrial capital and quasi-capital goods and miscellaneous items. About £S13.3 million (66.5%) of the minor donors' aid was extended between 1971 and 1976 (Denmark in 1971 and 1974, and France, Belgium and Japan in 1976). In addition to showing that new donors, albeit with small contributions, had come forward to assist Sudan's development efforts, the involvement of these countries also revealed Sudan's new policy towards Western capitalist assistance.

Aid from the Kingdon of the Netherlands

The case of Dutch aid exemplifies the aid principles and procedures of minor donors. As is true of the large and medium donors, Netherlands officials assert that their aid policy aims at promoting cordial relations with other countries on the basis of interdependence and mutual respect. Dutch bilateral capital aid is made available through the Netherlands Investment Bank for Developing Countries and the Netherlands Credit Insurance Company, Ltd., under government guarantees.[12] Technical Assistance includes a fellowship programme, a technical experts programme, the Netherlands peace corps, and expanded technical cooperation and the joint financing of private development projects.

12. Attachments and enclosures to a note from the Netherlands Embassy in Khartoum, entitled "the Netherlands and Technical Assistance" F/1935/67, page 2, Ministry of Foreign Affairs, Khartoum, File No. 9 (Netherlands).

TABLE 16
The volume and terms of capital aid commitments extended by Minor Western European Donors and Japan, 1962-1976 (£S million)*

source of aid	effective date	amount	annual interest rate	grace perior
Holland	1962	.3	5¾%	none
	1965	1.0	5½%	7 yrs
	1975	1.5	2½%	8 yrs
	1976	1.7	.75%	10 yrs
Sweden	1966	1.4	2%	10 yrs
	1970	1.0	2%	10 yrs
Denmark	1971	.7	none	17 yrs
	1974	1.2	none	10 yrs
Belgium	1976	1.8	7½%	3 yrs
France	1976	6.2	7½%	3 yrs
Japan	1969	3.8	6%	5 yrs
	1976	3.4	3%	10 yrs

* Ministry of National Planning, Khartoum, May 1977.

** A= Agriculture; In= Industry; TC= Transport and

maturity	repayment perior	withdrawals	benefiting sectors A	IN	TC	** CG
5 yrs	1962-1967	.3			X	
26 yrs	1972-1991	1.03				X
38 yrs	1983-2013	1.0				X
50 yrs	1986-2026	1.7				X
36 yrs	1976-1990	1.3	X			
25 yrs	1980-1994	0.9	X			
24 yrs	1988-1995	0.7	X			
34 yrs	1984-2008	1.1	X			
5 yrs	1979-1981	none			X	
9 yrs	1979-1986	none		X		
13 yrs	1974-1982					
30 yrs	1986-2006	none			X	

Communications; CG= Capital and quasi capital goods.

Sudan's relations with the Netherlands began when Sudan requested and Holland extended capital aid in 1962 for the purchase of six Fokkar Friendship airplanes. In 1965 Holland agreed to lend £S1 million as capital aid and technical assistance for expenses incurred in building a bridge on Bahr el-Jebel (White Nile) near Juba, and for technical training and feasibility studies on other projects. However, because of the civil war in the southern Sudan, the bridge was not built until 1975.

Another agreement on economic and technical cooperation was initialled in Khartoum on 19 June 1968, just three months after the 1967/68 Act on the Encouragement of Investment in the Sudan came into effect. One of the purposes of the agreement was to foster the inflow to the Sudan of Dutch private investment. Various provisions of the agreement promised guarantees of, and fair and equitable treatment for, such investment, but did not mention a specific amount of capital aid or designate any particular projects to be financed. However, as a result of the change of regime in the Sudan in 1969, the accord was not ratified until 1970.

Loans granted by the Netherlands between 1964 and 1976 amounted to less than £S5 million. The first two loans, in 1964 and 1965, were smaller, and had higher interest rates and shorter grace periods than later loans in 1975 and 1976. (See Table 16). The 1975 and 1976 aid equalled about 78% of all Dutch contributions to the Sudan between 1964 and 1976. The change in the terms and volume of aid in the mid-1970s resulted from the Netherlands government's 1975 decision to include

The Sudan among its "general target" countries receiving both programme and project aid annually. This decision may, in turn, have stemmed from the decline in Sudan's relations with the USSR and other Eastern European countries and its shift towards Western capitalist countries after the July 1971 coup attempt.

In addition to capital aid, the Netherlands has been extending technical assistance to the Sudan since the 1960s. An average of 50 to 60 Sudanese go to Holland each year, either as part of the Netherlands fellowships programme or to be educated as experts in various fields.

The Dutch firm Philips Telecommunication industries has implemented a number of major telecommunication projects in Sudan, such as the shortwave broadcasting transmitters at Soba, south of Khartoum, and the main Khartoum telephone exchange. These projects were financed either from the soft Dutch loan of £S1 million in 1965 or from finance-credits given by the Netherlands government. Some £S4 million were earmarked for various phases of these projects, including expenses incurred from the involvement of 14 Dutch experts Assisting in their execution and in the training of Sudanese counterparts. In the first decade of these projects, approximately 60 Sudanese were trained at the Philips International Telecommunications Training Centre.[13]

---

13. Memorandum of Dr. C.W. VanSanten, Deputy Legal Advisor of the Ministry of Foreign Affairs, the Hague, quoted in Ministry of Foreign Affairs, Khartoum, File No. 9 (Netherlands), pp. 149-155.

In the field of agriculture, there were intensive contacts between the University of Khartoum's Agricultural Institute at Shambat-Khartoum North and the Agricultural University of Wageningen intended to improve seed potato varieties. Several Sudanese undertook post-graduate studies in Wageningen. The Netherlands also offered fourteen metric tons of seed potatoes for agricultural experiments in the Jebel Marra area to promote the potato in the Sudan.

On 19 May 1970 the Agricultural Development Corporation of the Sudan and the Netherlands consulting firm ILACO signed an agreement for the "Tambul Pilot Farm Project". With a budget of £S1 million, this was the precursor of the giant Rahad Irrigation Scheme. The IBRD made available the foreign exchange component needed for the Tambul project and the Sudan Government requested the services of a Dutch economist to supervise the project and assist in drafting a Five Year Plan which would incorporate the Rahad Scheme. This was the 1970/71-1974/75 development plan. In the field of animal resources there was also close co-operation. As a token of friendship in June 1968, the Dutch Minister of Economy offered £S150,000 and technical assistance for the foundation of a school for animal husbandry technicians.

The Netherlands also aided the Sudan in the field of aviation. In 1964, the Sudan pioneered the use of the Fokker Friendship aircraft in Africa. Shortly after this transaction, the Sudan requested the Netherlands to conduct studies on the feasibility of modifying a dozen airfields to make them suitable for day and night operations. The Dutch authorities agreed and increased the allocation to £S500,000 for this study.

Finally, the Netherlands took an active interest in the development of the Piastre Technical Institute. On 17 June 1968, the Dutch Minister of Economic Affairs laid the foundation stone for a new building for the Institute which, on completion, enabled another hundred orphans to receive training in carpentry, smithing, and the like.

Sudan and Communist donors

Development assistance from Communist countries to developing countries is estimated at roughly 0.3% of the GNP of the USSR. the Eastern Europern countries, and China. This figure includes not only aid to non-communist developing countries, which has totalled less than 0.1% of GNP since it began in 1954, but also the much more substantial flow of resources of Communist developing countries which began seven years earlier.[14] Such assistance is not called "aid" in the Western capitalist sense, but is rather, termed "economic cooperation". The Communist countries have resisted pressure to do as many Western countries have done and commit a fixed percentage of their GNP to aid. They feel no obligation to reach the 1% target recommended by the OECD for development assistance to the Third World. The Communist countries argue that trade with less developed countries is more important than aid, but it must be borne in mind that some Communist donor countries are themselves developing countries if judged by such

---

14. OECD Observer, No. 46, June 1970, p. 36.

classical indicators as annual per capita income, GNP, balance of trade, and industrial development. The stated objective of Communist assistance is to strengthen the political and economic independence of the recipient nations by developing an economy no longer reliant on the old colonial structures. Given the conviction that these goals can best be achieved through industrialisation and the expansion of the state-owned sector of the economy, most activity would be socialist-oriented.

Sudan's major experiment with this approach was the rash, unplanned nationalisation of some foreign owned businesses and the confiscation of more than forty privately owned enterprises in 1970, which caused innumerable difficulties. The impact of the nationalisations was immediate. The inflow of capital from Western countries became negligible or ceased altogether. Only after £S12 million was agreed upon in compensation, mainly with Britain, was there a revival of Western activity.

The Communist states do not belong to the World Bank or participate in the World Food Programme, nor have they formed a similar multilateral organisation which extends wordwide development assistance independently of individual countries. Thus, in contrast to Western countries which contribute to multilateral aid organisations and offer bilateral aid at the same time, they offer exclusively bilateral assistance.

There are, generally speaking, marked differences between the kind of assistance provided by the Soviet Union and the Socialist countries of Eastern Europe on the one hand and the Peoples' Republic of China (PRC) on the other. The Soviet Union concentrates on heavy industry and infrastructure:about 70% of Soviet aid has benefited such industrial projects as the Bhilai and Bokhara steel works in India.[15] China has tended to emphasize immediately productive medium and small scale projects (short gestation period schemes), mainly in food processing, light industry, and infrastructure. Table 17 shows the main characteristics of aid to the Sudan from the centrally planned economies of Eastern Europe.

Starting as early as 1959 with Yugoslavia, the first Socialist country to extend aid to the Sudan, Communist states pledged about £S95 million until 1976, although only £S46.6 million (48%) has actually been expended. Three-quarters of these commitments came between 1969 and 1971, after the radical, pro-Communist military coup took place. £S28.2 million of Chinese commitments (about 30% of all Communist Commitments), however, came late in 1971, or soon after the alledgedly Russian instigated coup which caused a rupture in Sudanese-Soviet relations and led the Sudan to substitute China for the Soviet Union in its foreign aid quest.

There are differences between China and the other Communist countries regarding terms of assistance. Grants account for only a minor share of Soviet and Eastern European aid to non-Communist countries[16] and in the case of the Sudan, the records show no grants at all. Moreover, most Communist assistance consists

---

15. Lecture by the Chairman of the Soviet Committee of the USSR Council fo Ministers for External Economic Relations delivered in Moscow, 28 November, 1966, p.7. Ministry of Foreign Affairs, Khartoum, File No.9 (Soviet Union).

16. OECD Observer, No. 46, June 1970, p.36.

TABLE 17
The volume and terms of capital aid commitments extended by social countries, 1959-1971 (£S million)*

source of aid	effective date	amount	annual interest rate	grace period
Yugoslavia	1959	7.8	3%	
Czecho slovakia	1965	3.3	3%	2 yrs
	1973	7.0	3%	
USSR	1961		3½%	
	1969	2.0	2½%	4 yrs
Bulgaria	1968	5.0	2½%	
GDR	1969	4.0	2½%	3 yrs
Hungary	1970	3.5	2½%	3 yrs
Rumania	1972	25.0	2½%	2 yrs
North Korea	1970	1.3	None	1 yr
	1970	14.1	None	6 yrs
	1971	14.1	None	6 yrs

* Ministry of National Planning, khartoum, May 1976.

** ED= Education; In= Industry; TC= Transport and communications; CG= Capital and quasi capital goods.
* Repayment starts after completion of each contract;
** Repayment starts after last shipment;****** Repayment starts after execution of cash individual contract;

maturity	repayment period	withdrawals	benefiting sectors			
			ED	IN	TC	CG**
8 yrs	*	7.8		X	X	
8 yrs	1967-74	3.5		X		X
12 yrs	**	6.0		X		
15 yrs	1973-83	1.8				
8 yrs	***	0.4	X	X		
12 yrs	****	3.9				X
10 yrs	*****	3.5			X	
10 yrs	1974-82	0.9				
10 yrs	******	1.3				X
25 yrs	1976-95	14.1		X	X	
25 yrs	1987-96	0.3	X	X		

**** Repayment starts 3 years after date of shipment of goods; ***** Repayment starts 3 years after signature of contracts of purchase ****** Repayment starts one year after project becomes operational and continues for 10 years.

TABLE 18
A cross-section of total arab capital aid commitments, 1962-1976
(approximated to the nearest £S million)

source of aid	'62	'63	'64	'65	'66	'67	'68
Kuwait	6.8			1.7		4.9	
Saudi Arabia							
United Arab Emirates							
Libya							
Algeria						0.7	
Iraq							
Egypt						0.7	7.1
Arab Fund							
TOTAL	7			2		6.0	7

	'69	'70	'71	'72	'73	'74	'75	'76
	3.5		16.2	1.6	29.9	32.0	14.4	11.9
							9.7	12.8
								19.6
			3.4					
	6.0							
						9.6	8.8	15.7
	10		20	2	30	42	19	60

of development credits calling for repayment over 8-12 years at interest rates of 2½%-3% and with grace periods of 1-4 years. China, by contrast, offered interest free loans to the Sudan (and some grants in aid), with longer redemption periods (up to 25 years), and which were accompanied by considerable technical assistance, the costs of which the Chinese government usually bore. China was also keen to train counterparts, whether technicians or skilled labourers, to replace Chinese staff in the shortest possible time after the projects became operational.

Applying the criteria used earlier for classifying donors as major, medium, and minor, it is clear that, with the exception of China and Romania (medium donors), all Communist countries are minor donors. Czechoslovakia and the Soviet Union would become medium donors only if the credit facilities they extended in the period under consideration were added.

Almost all Communist aid accrued to the industrial sector, the transport sector, and the purchase of capital goods and equipment. Communist aid is linked to the procurement of goods and expert services from the donor country, although some triangular arrangements are possible. Loans from Communist countries are normally repaid either in goods from the recipient country (barter trade) or in the recipient's local currency, unless freely convertible currency has been specified.

Romania, in 1972, offered the largest capital aid loan of any Eastern European donor. It amounted to US 75 million dollars (£S25 million), and was repayable in kind within ten years at 2½% interest. Sudanese goods were exchanged for Romanian capital goods in biannual shipments, with 50% of the amount extended on ratification of the agreement and another 50% on submission of freight documents. This loan facilitated the extraction of iron-ore deposits at Jebel Abu-Tolo in Southern Kordofan Province; geological research on non-ferrous deposits; the exploitation of copper deposits in Southern Darfur Province; petroleum exploration; the establishment of a factory producing tanning and dyeing materials, and another for textile weaving, with a third for alcohol and yeast production from sugar-cane by-products; animal feed production; the production of seed oil and oil cakes; the promotion of the fishing industry; and the improvement of river transport systems.

Experts and research groups have been sent and some research has started. The Romanian authorities also agreed to the allocation of about US 12 million dollars of this loan to build a new complex for the People's Assembly in Omdurman and a weaving factory in Khartoum North. Although Romania only made this one loan, it constituted 26½% of the total capital aid commitments of all the Eastern European countries, China, and North Korea between 1956 and 1976.

The second largest of the Socialist donors was the People's Republic of China, which gave two loans in 1970 and 1971, each of £S14.1 million. Both were interest free, were repayable in 25 years, and had six years grace periods. They constituted a quarter of all Socialist and Communist aid and were utilized in the fields of agriculture, textiles, and transport, communications, and associated services. Withdrawals on these loans reached £S14.4 million, i.e. about 59.5% of the total amount. The 1970 loan was exhausted completely and only £S0.3 million of the second loan of 1971 had been withdrawn up to 1976. After Romania and China came Czechoslovakia with commitments of £S10.5 million; the USSR with £S10 million; Bulgaria with £S5 million; East Germany with £S4 million; Hungary with £S3.5 million; and North Korea with £S1.3 million.

Table 17 shows that £S67 million of £S95.3 million (about 70%) committed by Socialist countries between 1959 and 1976 came between 1969 and 1973. Aid extended during this time was often larger and offered on easier terms loans dating from before the 1969 d'etate.

Aid from Arab countries and finance institutions

Tables 18-21 show that the Sudan secured commitments of £S225 million from Arab countries and financial institutions between 1958 and 1976. The major bilateral Arab donors were Kuwait (£S122.6 million), the Kingdom of Saudi Arabia (£S39.5 million) and the United Arab Emirates (£S41 million). The only significant multilateral institution was the Arab Fund for Economic and Social Development, which began extending aid to the Sudan in 1974 and offered five loans totaling £S34 million. Minor Arab donors included Libya (£S6 million), Algeria (£S.7 million), Egypt (£S7.8 million), Qatar (£S4.6 million), and Iraq, which offered £S10 million to cover Sudan petroleum needs in 1974.

Table 18 indicates that Sudan started receiving Arab capital aid in 1962 in support of its Ten Year Plan. Contributions prior to 1971 were relatively small, while some 76% of all Arab aid given to the Sudan came between 1971 and 1976. Roughly a third of this aid entered the agricultural sector, another third went to transport and communications, 16% was earmarked for the industrial sector, and the remainder benefited other sectors of the economy. Some Arab loans, including six from Saudi Arabia, consisted of hard cash to strengthen

TABLE 19
The volume and terms of capital aid commitments extended by Kuwait, 1962-1976 (£S million)*

effective date	amount	annual interest rate	grace period	maturity	repayment period	withdrawals	benefiting sector A	IN	TC	** CG
1962	6.8	4%	4 yrs	11 yrs	1966-73	6.6			X	
1965	1.7	3½%	3 yrs	7 "	1968-72	1.7		X		
1967	4.9	2½%	3 yrs	21 "	1970-88	4.9	X			
1969	2.2	8%	2 yrs	5 "	1971-74	2.2				
1969	1.3	8%	none	4 "	1969-73	1.3				
1971	16.2	2%	5 yrs	8 "	1976-79	16.2	X			
1972	1.6	2½%	5 yrs	24 "	1977-96	0.7	X			
1973	4.4	2½%	5 yrs	16 "	1978-89	4.4		X		
1973	17.2	2½%	5 yrs	30 "	1978-2008		X			
1973	8.3	8½%	4 yrs	11 "	1977-84	8.3		X		
1974	32.0	8½%					X			
1975	17.2	2½%	5 yrs	30 "	1978-2008		X			
1975	12.5	8½%	2 yrs	12 "	1977-85	14.5		X		
1975	1.9	4%	5 yrs	16 "	1980-91	1.9		X		
1976	1.1	1½%	10 yrs	40 "	1986-2015	-				
1976	10.8	3%	7 yrs	22 "	1983-98	-				X

* Ministry of National Planning, Khartoum, May 1976.

** A= Agriculture; IN= Industry; TC= Transportation and Communication; CG= Capital and quasi-capital goods.

Sudan's balance of payments.

Aid from Kuwait

Kuwait was one of the first countries to assist Sudan with its first Ten Year Plan. Kuwait initially committed and paid out foreign aid through special agencies and state reserves, although the National Assembly came to oppose loans from the latter source. The Kuwait Fund for Arab Economic Development (KFAED), established in 1961 is the aid giving institution. KFAED follows lending practices which have always been influenced by the business-like practices of the older, more established international institutions, particula-rly the IBRD. It adheres to strict criteria in determ-ining the credit worthiness of recipient countries and the projects for which financing has been requested.

KFAED is a project, rather than programme, lender. It charter requires it to ascertain the priority rating of individual projects whithin the recipient country's development plans and to consider the return on invest-ments. To do this, missions investigate the financial and economic aspects, as well as the technical feasi-bility, of projects under consideration. In theory, KFAED avoids loans for projects which might lead to duplication or prove obstacles to economic plans on the regional level, although these restrictions are not al-ways observed. Important stipulations of the charter protect the lender's interests by obliging the borrower to furnish KAFED with adequate information on the pro-gress of the project throughout the maturity period and having the borrower agree to the exemption of KAFED's assets from all domestic taxes and duties as well as from nationalisation or confiscation. Moreover, to achieve an effective role for local capital, KAFED limits its participation in any project to no more than half the financial requirements.

Four major policies characterize the fund.[17] First, there is an emphasis on infrastructure projects. In the case of the Sudan, as illustrated in Table 19, 59% of Kuwait's aid went to the agricultural sector, 24% to industry, 15% to transportation and communications, and only 2% to other sectors and services. The stress on agriculture, especially after 1971 when Kuwait began making larger loans than previously, resulted from the Arabs' desire to develop their agricultural potential to prevent possible political coercion or blackmail from other countries and from a policy of enhancing alternative food sources in the expectation that petroleum reserves will diminish in the future.

Secondly, since the 1970s, KFAED has tended to make loans for agriculture and agro-industries rather than other types of industrial development. After phasing out loans provided for small projects, the fund concentrated on larger ventures, as may be seen in Sudan's case. Prior to 1971, small loans were given away every two years for minor projects, or to meet part of the cost of large projects financed by primarily a third party, as in the case of the Khashm el-Girba sugar project. In this instance, West Germany was the main contributor, but supplemental loans were needed for expenses over and above German commitments.

A third feature is KFAED's enthusiasm for projects with regional implications, such as Sudan Railways and the deepening of the Suez Canal. Fourth, and possibly most important in the long run, are the reasonable terms

---

17. Ministry of Foreign Affairs, Khartoum, File No. 9 (Kuwait). This file is in Arabic. Translations of its main points have been made by this writer.

of the loans. KAFED usually charges a flexible rate of interest from three to four per cent below that prevailing in the recipient country, with an average maturity of 19 years. The repayment schedule provides for low interest charges in the early years of the project which can be increased as the project begin to produce revenue. On the whole, KFAED's lending terms compare favourably with those of donors in the Development Assistance committee, "BAC" of the OECD, whose interest rates average about 5% and are almost in line with those of us A.I.D. (3½% and 20 years maturity).

In the period from 1962 to 1976 Kuwaiti foreign aid agencies extended fifteen loans to the Sudan amounting to £S122 million. Their interest rates varied between 2% and 8½%. Loans from government reserves had low interest rates of between 2½% and 4%, while those from semi-government institutions carried higher rates (8½%) and had shorter redemption periods. The smallest loan was for £S1.6 million in 1972; the highest in 1974 amounted to £S32 million. The annual average Kuwaiti capital entering the Sudan has been about £S9 million. The loans extended between 1962 and 1967 averaged £S4.6 million, with none exceeding £S5 million. Assistance decreased between 1967 and 1971, but some loans between 1971 and 1976 reached more than £S30 million. The annual average in this latter period was about £S11 million. The resumption of Kuwaiti aid in 1971 came only one month after the Communist inspired coup attempt was foiled, and the falling off of Kuwaiti aid may be attributed to concerns over the deteriorating political situation in the southern Sudan between 1964 and 1968, political turmoil in the north, and the 1969 change in the political system. 1969-1971 saw a general decline

TABLE 20
The volume and terms of capital aid commitments extended by Saudi Arabia and the United Arab Emirates, 1971-1976

source of aid	effective date	amount	annual interest rate	grace period	maturity	repayment period	withdrawals	benefiting sector		
								A	IN	TC
Saudi Arabia**		3.3	5%							
		4.5	5%							
		4.5	5%							
		4.4	7½%							
		3.3								
	1975	9.7	3%	5 yrs	25 yrs	1980–2000	1.6	X		
	1976	3.6	2%	6 yrs	20 yrs	1982–1996	3.6	X		X
	1976	9.2	2%	6 yrs	20 yrs	1982–1997	9.2			X
United Arab Emirates	1971	3.5	2½%	5 yrs	10 yrs	1976–1981	3.5			X
		8.0								X
		10.0								
	1976	6.4	5%	3 yrs	12 yrs	1979–1988	5.8		X	
	1976	13.2	3%	6 yrs	20 yrs	1982 1997		X		

* Ministry of National Planning, Khartoum, May 1976.

** The first five items were cash loans, offered in the sequence noted.

in foreign aid from capitalist countries and Arab states and closer relations with Communist Eastern Europe and China.

87% of Kuwaiti's foreign aid to the Sudan came in the years 1971-1976, much of it channelled into joint ventures and joint investment entities. In 1973, the Sudanese-Kuwaiti Investment Company was established with headquarters in Khartoum, a paid-up capital of £S1million, and a shared control, with 51% for the Sudan government and 49% for the Kuwaiti government. The company utilises, explores, and exploits Sudan's natural resources by constructing factories and promoting trade.[18] Other areas of Kuwaiti investments include the construction of the Khartoum Hilton Hotel and the Al-Qarabeen Village agricultural project.

Kuwait also extended grants to the Sudan, most of which covered feasibility studies in the fields of transport, sugar plants, grain storage, and livestock developments. In 1973 a grant of £S1.2 million allowed for a comprehensive feasibility study of the transport sector done under contract by American experts. The ILO's report on Sudan's development strategy for the rest of the 20th century later incorporated their detailed plan.

After the settlement of the southern problem, Kuwait, along with many other countries, extended aid and grants to assist in resettlement and rehabilitation efforts. In 1973, US 1 million dollars was earmarked for building roads and reconstructing hospitals, mosques and schools in the southern region. An office staffed by three Kuwaitis was established in Juba to supervise the project. In January 1975, the Vice-President of the Sudan, Mr Abel Alier, visited Kuwait and

18. Ibid.

requested US 2 million dollars for the purchase of agricultural equipment and capital goods for road construction in the south, to which Kuwait agreed. This was the first instance of a high ranking southern official visiting a foreign country to ask for bilateral aid, although an attempt had been made the previous year to obtain multilateral aid when a delegation visited the IBRD seeking funds for rehabilitation and resettlement in the south.[19]

Kuwaiti-Sudanese aid relations can be used to exemplify a common statistical problem. Sudanese officials prepared a report for the guidance of a delegation holding talks with Kuwaiti aid representatives in 1975.[20] In a section on Kuwaiti economic relations with Sudan the report noted that in 1974 Kuwait had allocated US 80 million dollars through an agreement between the Kuwaiti Trading, Contracting, and Foreign Investment Company and Sudan's Cotton Marketing Company to facilitate the marketing of Sudanese cotton. However, the records at the Ministry of National Planning and the Department of Statistics, the official custodians of such data, do not mention this large export facility, nor does the report itself mention the terms under which it was extended. Occasionally, records and statistics are contradictory. The previously mentioned report indicated that Sudan received two loans in August 1971, of KD 10 million and KD 6 million. The first was to cover government expenditure in sugar wheat; the second was for the purchase of consumer goods. KD 16 million is equivalent to approximately £S25 million. Planning

---

19. Interview with Mr. Sappana Jambo, Regional Director for Planning in the Southern Region, Juba, January 1977.

20. Ministry of Foreign Affairs, Khartoum, File No. 9 (Kuwait), pp. 30-47.

commission statistics, however, show that 1971 loans totaled only £S16.2 million. It is impossible to say why these discrepancies exist, but there are similar problems regarding loans from Saudi Arabia prior to 1975.

Aid from Saudi Arabia and the United Arab Emirates

Table 20 gives a somewhat distorted view of Saudi capital assistance to the Sudan in that official statistics and tables issued up to May 1977 show only three Saudi loans amounting to £S21.5 million. The five other loans cited in the table are mentioned in the 1974 Economic Survey[21] in the sequence noted in the footnotes. (No mention is made of a first loan). Thus, Saudi Arabia extended six cash loans of £S29 million before 1975 and three project loans in 1975-1976, bringing "acknowledged aid" to a total of £S51 million. Ministry of Foreign Affairs statistics differ substantially from those of the Planning Commission and the Ministry of National Planning in 1975 and 1977 respectively. A report on economic co-operation between Sudan and Saudi Arabia listed capital aid extended in the form of loan and bank deposits from various Saudi finance institutions to help strengthen Sudan's serious balance of payments problem.[22] The list included:

1. The Saudi National Commercial Bank; a loan of SR 40 million.
2. ZALOUKH Bank:a loan of US 15 million dollars.
3. Jameen Bank:a loan of US 4.5 million dollars.

---

21. 1974 Economic Survey, National Planning Commission, Khartoum, 1975. Appendix Table 6-4, pp. 220.

22. Ministry of Foreign Affairs, Khartoum, File No. 9 (Saudi Arabia).

TABLE 21
The volume and terms of capital aid commitments extended by Minor Arab donors and the Arab Fund, 1969-1976

source of aid	amount	annual interest rate	grace period	maturity period	repayment period	withdrawals	A	IN	TC
Libya	6.05	2½% above British T/B				6.05	X	X	
Algeria	.71	None				.71			
Iraq	10.0								
Egypt	.73	None	6 yrs	30 yrs	1973-1996	.73	X		
	7.1	None	5 yrs		5 yrs from each insurance policy				
Qatar	4.6	5%							
Arab Fund	9.6	4%	6 yrs	20 yrs	1980-94	3.2			X
	5.7	4%	5 yrs	20 yrs	1980-95	2.8			X
	3.1	2½%	3 yrs	20 yrs	1980-93	-			X
	3.2	4%	7 yrs	20 yrs	1983-97	-			X
	2.5	5%	4 yrs	7 yrs	1981-83	-			X

* Ministry of National Planning, Khartoum, May 1976.

4. The Saudi Arabian Monetary Establishment: a guarantee to the Sudan enabling it to secure a loan of US 200 million dollars from a consortium of Western European banks. This loan served as paid-up capital for the establishment of the Sudanese Development Corporation. The Monetary Establishment also deposited US 150 million dollars for the Sudan.

Moreover, the Saudi Development Fund, established in 1974, allocated US 100 million dollars in March 1975 to finance the following Sudanese development projects:

1. US 28.8 million dollars for Rahad Project.
2. US 20 million dollars for Port Sudan Airport.
3. US 26 million dollars for Kassala-Haya Road.
4. US 25.2 million dollars for Nyala-Kas - Zalingi.

Only the first three of these loans are mentioned in the Planning Commission records.

The Arabian Company for Investment contributed to the financing of Kenana sugar factory and the microwave network in the country. Saudi Arabia also assisted in building the African Islamic Centre in Khartoum and the Islamic Centre in Juba, in the construction of mosques in different parts of the country, and in meeting current expenditure at Omdurman Islamic University. Such conflicting statistics cast doubts on the accuracy of information regarding other donors.

Data on aid from the United Arab Emirates is also bedeviled by the same problems and information about all loans is incomplete. It is clear, however, that most aid from the UAE went to the transport and communications sector, was extended at a low rate of interest (3%), and had medium maturity periods (between 10 and 20 years).

The Libyan Loan

In a period of good relations between the Sudan and Libya, the countries signed a loan agreement in November 1969, just two months after the successful coup d'etat brought Colonel Mummar Kadafi to power in Tripoli. The terms of the agreement stated that the Arab Republic of Libya would extend £S6.05 million to the Sudan as an investment in Sudan's development projects and in the banking operations of the Sudanese Agricultural and Industrial banks.

£S1.67 million, repayable in two equal installments were allocated to the Agricultural Bank under Sudan government guarantee. The due date of the first installment was the end of the third year from the date of actual withdrawal of the bank's share; the second installment coming due one year later. Another £S1.67 million went to the Industrial Bank, again under government guarantee, with the same repayment arrangement. The Sudan government had the option of extending the due date of the first installment of each loan up to five years. The remaining £S2.71 million was for development projects. It was repayable in three installments, the first a year after the withdrawal of the loan, the second one a year later, and the third a year after that.

The agreement specified the rate of interest as 2% less than the rate for international money on each due date. The Foreign Loans Section of the Ministry of Planning figured the principal and interest on this loan as follows:

Due Date	Principal (£S)	Interest	Total
24.11.70	836,800	242,000	1,070,800
1971 - 72	836,800	208,620	1,045,420
1972 - 73	1,044,000	160,250	1,204,250

"On November 27, 1969", according to Arab Report and Record, "President Nimeiri reported that Sudan had received a Libyan loan of £S7.25 million at 2% interest".[23] This statement contradicts the figures just cited and is a case of the president "politicking" with foreign aid and disseminating information which did not agree with that released by his aides and specialized Government units. The first such incident had occurred at the inauguration of the Five Year Plan. This behaviour confirms that publicity about foreign aid frequently ignores its important technical aspects while embellishing its political aspects. Actual aid negotiations are extremely businesslike affairs, often involving subtle calculations. They may not always be governed by complete economic rationality, but they are far more complex than public relations images of them that are sometimes presented.

During a period of strained relations between Sudan and Libya in 1974, the Sudanese President revealed that Libya had requested Sudan to return an earlier loan which had been made during happier days "from one fraternal revolution to another as a loan which needn't be repaid". Sudan's Minister of Information described the demand as a "national insult" and announced the formation of a Committee for the Defence of Sudan's Dignity which would find ways of publicly collecting funds to repay the Libyan loan. The President himself said:

> As we all know, we do not accept charity nor do we accept superiority; we do not agree that bread should deprive us of dignity, even if we have to starve to death...[24]

---

23. Arab Report and Record, 1969, p. 494.
24. Foreign Broadcast Information Service, 12 June 1974.

This episode makes it clear that it is not only the big powers which use economic aid as a means of political coercion. Small but wealthy countries are not beyond manipulating aid relations to serve their political interests if circumstances lend themselves to such action.

Multilateral Aid

Along with the proliferation of bilateral aid programmes in recent decades, multilateral institutions have also grown increasingly important. The 1944 bretton Woods Conference resulted not only in a new international monetary system with the International Monetary Fund as its capstone but also in a companion organization, the International Bank for Reconstruction and Development, a lending institution designed to tap private financial markets. The World Bank group includes a soft loan subsidiary, the International Development Association (IDA), established in 1960, and an equity financing affiliate, the International Finance Corporation (IFC), begun in 1956.[25]

There are a number of multilateral institutions providing significant technical assistance to developing countries or supplementing the capital sources of the big banks. The most important is the United Nations system, a vast and complicated web of more than 30 administrative units.[26] There are three basic types of

---

25. For a historical account of the World Bank group, see Edward S. Maeen and Robert E. Asher, The World Bank Since Bretton Woods. (Washington D.C.:Brookings Institution), 1973.

26. Officially, the World Bank group is part of the UN system, but in practice it is quite autonomous. For a comprehensive analysis of the economic and social functions of the UN system, see Mahdi Elmandjra, The United Nations System:An Analysis (Hamden, Connecticut, Archon Books), 1973.

United Nations organisations that play a role in development assistance: the special funds, the executing or specialized agencies, and the regional commissions. The special funds include the United Nations Development Programme (UNDP), the United Nations Fund for Population Activities (UNFPA), the United Nations Children's Fund (UNICEF), and the United Nations Environmental Programme (UNEP). These special funds conduct some of their own technical assistance operations, but most of their resources are channelled through specialised or executing agencies, such as the Food and Agricultural Organisation (FAO), the International Labour Organisation (ILO), the World Health Organization (WHO), the United Nations Educational, Scientific, and Cultural Organisation (UNESCO), the United Nations Idustrial Development Organisation (UNIDO), and the United Nations Conference on Trade and Development (UNCTAD). The regional Economic Commissions for Asia and the Far East (EFACE), for Latin America (ECLA), and for Africa (ECA), undertake research, coordinate efforts among their member countries, and provide advice and technical expertise in the scientific, educational and economic fields.

There are also smaller, regionally oriented, development banks which have expanded their operations in recent years. These include the aid institutions of the European Economic Community, the Caribean Development Bank (CDB), the African Development Bank (ADB), the African Development Fund (ADF), and others.

A major development in the 1960s was the growth of consortia, consulting groups, and other forms of bilateral and multilateral aid coordination. The term aid consortium is usually applied to groups of donors who meet and make formal pledges to provide assistance for a particular recipient country. Consulting groups of aid donors do not usually make formal pledges of assistance.

The main sources of multilateral aid to the Sudan have been the World Bank, the African Development Fund, and the Arab financial institutions. The United Nations also extends aid to the Sudan through specialized agencies and organisations. The contributions of these donors constituted 54.82% (£S346.6 million) of all capital aid commitments made to the Sudan between 1958 and 1976.[27] According to the Ministry of National Planning, multilateral aid has been used more efficiently than other kinds of aid. Officials at the Ministry attribute this to three main causes. First, these donors conduct careful feasibility studies and socio-economic analyses of the proposed project and its possible impact on the population of the area in which it is to be executed. Secondly, equipment required for the project is purchased through international tenders, thereby providing the most suitable technology for Sudan's environment at the most reasonable free market prices. Finally, officials of the multilateral institutions make on the job inspections and field visits to monitor the progress of the project and eliminate problems as they arise through cooperation with local counterparts. Ministry of National Planning officials also believe that the Sudan's capacity for absorbing multilateral aid is sufficiently high to warrent giving serious consideration to developing a national policy of cooperation with these institutions

Table 22 considers two international financial institutions (IBRD and African Development Bank) as examples of multilateral donors. The IBRD first came to

---

27. Ministry of National Planning, op. cit., p. 1.

TABLE 22
The volume and terms of capital aid commitments extended by multilateral aid institutions, 1958-1976
(£S million)

source of aid	effective date	amount	annual interest rate	grace period
IBRD	1958	13.6	$5\frac{1}{8}$%	3 yrs
	1960	5.4	6%	3 yrs
	1961	6.8	5½%	7 yrs
	1961	4.5		10 yrs
	1965	10.8	6½%	5 yrs
	1968	1.9	6½%	20 yrs
	1968	2.9		20 yrs
	1968	6.6	6½%	6 yrs
	1972	3.9	None	10 yrs
	1972	2.4	None	10 yrs
	1973	14.6	None	8 yrs
	1973	1.4	None	10 yrs
	1974	8.4	None	10 ysr
	1974	3.7	None	10 yrs
	1975	7.0	None	10 yrs
	1975	3.5	None	10 yrs
	1975	8.0	None	10 yrs
	1975	2.4	None	10 yrs
	1976	3.1	None	10 yrs
	1976	1.4	None	10 yrs
	1976	7.0	4.85%	5 yrs
ADB and ADF	1971	0.3	6%	None
	1971	1.0	6%	3 yrs
	1974	1.2	6%	3 yrs
	1974	1.5	6%	5 yrs
	1974	1.5	None	10 yrs
	1976	2.0	None	10 yrs

maturity	repayment period	withdraw-als	A	ED	EE	IR	IN	TC
			benefiting sector					
20 yrs	1968-1978	13.6						X
20 yrs	1963-1980	5.4	X					
25 yrs	1966-1986	6.8				X		
50 yrs	1971-2011	4.5				X		
25 yrs	1970-1990	10.8						X
50 yrs	1987-2018	1.9	X					
50 yrs	1987-2018	1.3	X		X			
25 yrs	1973-1993	6.6			X			
50 yrs	1981-2022	1.5	X					
50 yrs	1981-2022	2.2						X
50 yrs	1981-2023	4.6	X			X		
50 yrs	1984-2023	1.4					X	
50 yrs	1984-2024	7.7						X
50 yrs	1984-2024	.7	X					
50 yrs	1985-2025	5.4		X				
50 yrs	1985-2025	.4		X				
50 yrs	1985-2025	2.3		X		X		
50 yrs	1985-2025	.02					X	
50 yrs	1986-2026	-						X
50 yry	1986-2026	-						
45 yry	1983-2001	-						X
10 yrs	1971-1982	.25	X					
13 yrs	1974-1984	1.0						X
	1977-1987	.8						X
15 yrs	1978-1989			X				
50 yrs	1984-2024	.4						X
50 yrs	1986-2026	-			X			

Sudan's assistance in 1958. It extended 21 loans between 1958 and 1976 amounting to £S118.8 million, of which only £S77 million (64%) was actually withdrawn. Eight loans totalling £S50 million involved annual interest rates which averaged 6½%. The largest of these loans was also the first. Granted in 1958, it was for £S13.6 million, with an interest rate of 5 1/8%. The remaining loans came from IBRD's soft loan agency (IDA) and carried a service charge of ¾%, but were interest free. 38% of World Bank funds went to transport and communications, 31% to agriculture, 22% to irrigation, 3% to industry, and the remaining 6% to such other sectors as education and electric energy.

Six IDA credits and IBRD loans totalling US 106 million dollars had benefited Sudanese agriculture by the end of 1974. Money was spent on the Managil extension to the Gezira irrigation scheme (1960), Roseiris Dam (1966), the first mechanized farming scheme (1968 and 1972) and Rahad Irrigation scheme (1973). The southern region agricultural rehabilitation programme, a four year programme to revive agriculture, livestock, and forestry in the region, also received US 10.7 million dollars in 1974. The estimated economic rates of return were expected to vary from 10% to 27% for the individual programme components while the overall economic rate of return was estimated at 18%.

The African Development Bank (ADB) extended the Sudan loans amounting to £S 7.5 million, some 57% of which came directly from the African Development Bank, with the rest donated by the African Development Fund. ADB's loans are at 6% annual interest with redemption period varying between ten and fifteen years and grace periods of two to five years. Loans were given by ADB for the transport sector, animal health, and electrical energy. The ADF extended an interest free loan in 1974 for road construction and another for the development of a water supply project for Port Sudan. These loans were repayable in 40 years, after 10 years of grace.

United Nations aid is wholly in the form of grants and is also quite specific and project oriented. It focuses primarily on training, research, education, health and social services. Much of it goes to the public sector and, while its exact distribution cannot be gauged, Table 23 attempts to calculate its sectoral distribution.

United Nations aid falls into three categories: an expanded programme of technical assistance; aid from the United Nations Special Fund, with special UN agencies acting as executors; and direct aid from particular UN agencies. All of these forms provide for equipment, experts, and the training of counterparts. Tables 23 and 24 indicate that a large part of Un aid goes to equipment, underlining a substantial qualitative difference between UN aid and other aid. A primary apsect of UN aid is its non-political nature - a characteristic it shares with aid from other multilateral institutions, although there are shadings of the term "non-political".

Sudan's experience with United Nations aid and technical assistance programm's dates from 1954 when the world body provided £S15000. Three years later the UN appointed a resident representative in Khartoum to look into Sudan's needs. Table 23 shows that the United Nations Development Programme provided the Sudan with technical assistance valued at £S17.7 million between 1958 and 1976. Law ebb for UNDP aid came in 1959 and

1965, with high points in 1961, 1968, and 1972. £S3.07 million of UNDP's assistance (17.5%) entered the Sudan between 1958 and 1964 - during the first military regime of General Ibrahim Abboud. The largest amount during that period (£S1 million) came in 1961, at the time of the inauguration of the Ten Year Plan which attracted not only bilateral aid, but multilateral aid and technical assistance as well. Between 1965 and 1968, the Sudan received UNDP technical assistance amounting to £S3.6 million, or 20.3% of all UNDP assistance until 1976. The remaining 61.2% (£S11.2 million) dates from 1969-1976.

As shown in Table 23, UNDP intended most of its assistance to the Sudan to be shared by more than one economic sector. Of 19 loans, four went exclusively to the service sector, while the agricultural sector, the transport and communications sector, and the industrial sectors shared the rest.

The United Nations World Food Programme was established to provide food and assistance to poor countries so as to enable them to utilize their own resources - which they would otherwise have expended in the purchase of food and medicine - for economic and social development. The Sudanese agricultural sector received assistance from the World Food Programme for the control of the Nile sudd and the development of forestry. The World Food Programme also assisted in the field of primary and secondary education, technical education, and vocational training; participated in the resettlement residents of the Wadi Halfa in the Khashm el-Girba area; and helped with the rehabilitation of southern returnees after the Addis Ababa Agreement in 1972. Table 24 shows that the World Food Programme extended commitments of £S23.9 million in 1970 and 1976.

TABLE 23
Value of technical assistance extended by UNDP between 1958 and 1976*

year	amount in £S thousand	benefiting sector S	A	TC	IN
1958	182,916	X			
1959	68,450	X			
1960	432,915	X	X		
1961	1,085,378	X	X		X
1962	595,687	X	X	X	
1963	261,591	X	X		
1964	441,185	X	X		
1965	71,673	X			
1966	378,093	X			
1967	1,471,186	X	X		X
1968	1,654,328	X	X	X	X
1969	270,740	X	X		X
1970	1,606,388	X	X	X	
1971	2,240,680	X	X		X
1972	2,455,319	X	X	X	X
1973	1,806,760	X	X	X	X
1974	2,224,939	X	X	X	X
1975	492,839	X	X		
1976	68,340	X	X		
TOTAL	17,769,365				

* Ministry of National Planning, op. cit., p. 51.

TABLE 24
Value of "assistance in kind" extended by the United Nations World Food Programme Between 1970 and 1976 (£S million)

year	amount
1970-71	2,552,364
1971-72	2,658,544
1972-73	2,488,426
1973,74	2,650,505
1974,75	2,776,326
1975-76	4,053,513
1976- March '77	1,113,992
1977-78 (Projected)	5,569,417
TOTAL	23,862,087

* Ministry of National Planning, op. cit., p. 50.

AID FROM THE UNITED STATES OF AMERICA AND THE UNITED KINGDOM

By

Abdel Basit Saeed

For the American government, foreign aid is an instrument of foreign policy, whose purpose is to promote development. Development is not, however, an end in itself, but rather a means for establishing and maintaining political regimes characterized as "free", democratic", friendly to the United States, and in agreement with U.S. policies. Political security and economic stability are the aims of development aid. Another fundamental tenet of American aid is that it is given to end aid. Two additional features distinguish American aid programmes from those of other donors: a strong representation in the recipient country and an emphasis on self-help.[1] Because of these policies, U.S. officials scrutinize economic performance criteria; the preparation of development plans; forms of land tenure and tax structure; fiscal and institutional plans to raise domestic savings; and monetary policies avoiding quantitative restrictioning and giving scope for private investment. Final recommendations are often made in accordance with IBRD and IMF suggestions. American aid is administered by the Agency for International Development, which operates on an annual authorization and appropriation basis. Thus, funds must be provided each year for new activities or the extension or continuation of existing projects whose funding

1. Paul Steeten; Aid to Africa, August 1970. p. 19 (this is a report by the O.A.U.'s ECA to the 5th Joint ECA/OAU Meeting on Trade and Development.

has been expended. After receiving its funds from the Congress, AID enters into a variety of activities including technical assistance, development loans, (United Nations Development programmes), disaster and relief operations, assistance in training foreign students. AID assistance consists of two types of loans: project loans for specified capital projects and lines of credit to developing countries for the importation of commodities, equipment, or services for non-project development programmes.

American foreign aid plays a crucial role in the promotion of American exports. Between 1964 and 1969, goods financed by the Foreign Assistance Act constituted from 22% to 30% of all cargo moving on United States flag vessels. In fiscal year 1971, U.S. foreign aid channeled through AID made up 7% of all American exports to developing countries. AID financed exports in 1972 totalled $972 million - 23% of all American exports. looking at specific industries, in 1971 AID financed

- 16.4% of all U.S. exports of iron and steel products;
- 25% of all U.S. exports of fertilisers;
- 15.7% of all U.S. exports of railroad equipmnnt;
- 8% of all U.S. exports of rice;
- 8.5% of all U.S. exports of basic textiles; and
- 7.3% of all U.S. exports of non-ferrous metal products.[2] Other industries benefiting from exports through AID were petrochemicals; pulp and paper; motor vehicles and parts; electric machinery and machine tools.

In 1972, AID expenditures exceeded $3 billion, broken down as follows:

2. Steeton, ibid.

Development loans	US $ 1922.2 million
Technical assistance	212.4
Population	121.4
UN and other multilateral programmes	158.4
American schools and hospitals	26.9
Administrative expenses	9.8
Subtotal, development assistance	2500.0
Supporting assistance	704.2
Total	US $ 3204.2 million

It is not only the need of the poor countries, but also a desire to maximize profits in the industrial world, that give rise to the foreign aid phenomenon. Thus, it is not always an effective instrument for aiding developing countries and can be a clever method for exploiting them. The developed countries are not so irrational as to give away billions of dollars without ensuring that every dollar brings not only a financial profit but also such non-economic returns as a feeling of gratitude to the donor and the pacification of anti-imperialist forces which may oppose the domination of third world countries by a few rich industrial countries.

That the national interest of the United States is served by foreign aid contributions can be further illustrated by considering the costly political and economic repercussions for American industry, the American domestic market, and foreign trade of the suspension of such assistance. For instance, if AID lets a contract to an American manufacturer and funds are subsequently suspended, the manufacturer faces loss of payment, and without another market for the equipment, additional serious losses. Clearly, U.S. industry has a vested interest in the continuance of foreign aid to guarantee its income, markets abroad, and profit. The elimination of AID financing would adversely effect, along with the U.S. industries in various export areas, the U.S. shipping industry, other trade activities, and political decision making.

As for the developing countries, the suspension of a loan endangers the progress already realised under the loan and also disrupts the general process of development in the recipient country. For example, if AID signs a loan agreement to finance the import of breeding stock to improve the cattle industry in a developing country, the recipient government would be likely to invest large sums in such ancillary services as slaughter houses, freezing plants, transport, and feed mill facilities. Without the delivery of the commodities stated in the loan agreement the project will not give the results it was designed to realize and both the donor and the recipient stand to suffer, with potential strains in their political relations.

U.S. foreign aid is sometimes effectively applied as a means of political pressure on the recipient country. Table 1 reveals a vast difference between the amount of aid received by Egypt and three other African countries. This was not because Egypt was friendlier to the United States than the others, since Egypt had been hostile to the United States since the 1956 Suez Crisis. After a record high in 1965, American aid to Egypt declined to almost nothing in 1967, with the suspension of funds after the Arab-Israeli war in June. Political developments in the Middle East and the behaviour of Egypt and its Arab partners in the war, including the severance of diplomatic relations with the United States, led the American government to use foreign aid as an element of pressure against Egypt. The flow of foreign aid capital to developing countries sometimes depends on political relationships and the degree to which the recipients are involved in regional issues in a manner of which the donor country disapproves.

Table 1: Official flows to some African recipients of U. S. Aid, 1960-67 (approximated to nearest US $ million)

Country	1960	1961	1962	1963	1964	1965	1966	1967
U.A.R.*	113	115	117	174	168	86	51	1
Ethiopia	8	14	13	19	9	11	21	12
Ghana	2	2	2	13	8	33	62	33
Sudan	16	17	11	9	9	9	2	5

* includes grants to Syria during 1960.

Source: OECD Geographical distribution of financial flows to less developed countries, 1960-64, 1965 and 1966-67.

Despite the philosophical, or moral, and humanitarian rationales for the transfer of finance capital to developing countries espoused by the industrial world, foreign aid is neither a mindless give-away, nor merely an act of generosity. The politics of foreign aid have always been shrewdly calculated to achieve certain major objectives: serving the donor's economic, political, and military interests; and enhancing the donor's image at both the international and domestic levels.

The Sudan has not been exempt from these policies in its foreign aid and trade transactions since independence. The United States suspended aid to the Sudan in 1967 after the June War. The difference in the amount of aid given the Sudan and Egypt before 1967 stemmed from the strategic importance of the two countries to the United States. Egypt, as the military and economic spearhead of the Arab world, commanded more aid. Sudan was not important to American interests in Africa and exerted less influence on the Middle East situation.

It is not only finance capital which can be used to influence recipient countries. The United States has used food aid (and the USSR military aid) as means of acquiring leverage against Egypt. In 1965, for example, the New York Times reported that the United States was about to enter into a new aid agreement with Egypt which would require Egypt to pay part of its purchases of American food shipments in hard currency or through commercial barter deals to help combat the American balance-of-payment problems: "Aid talks, following congressional urgings to prohibit or greatly limit aid to Egypt, resulted in a grant of funds for the new arrangements which was smaller and of shorter duration than in the past".[3]

This helps to explain the sharp decline in American aid for Egypt between 1964 and 1965. In 1966 President Nasser declared: "the freedom we have bought with our blood, we shall not sell for wheat, for rice, or for anything".[4]

While some countries under duress may ask for and appreciate American aid, they nevertheless strongly resist the overt use of food aid or capital aid as a weapon of political or economic coercion.

---

3. New York Times, October 13, 1965.

4. Stephen Rosenfeld, "The Politics of Food", in Foreign Policy, no 14, Spring 1974, p.24.

Food Aid and American Foreign Policy

Since the Second World War, American agricultural productivity has been linked to foreign policy issues. Because of its natural endowment, modern technology, and sophisticated methods, the United States has long been capable of producing far more agricultural commodities than it consumes. Since the Great Depression, the American farm bloc has been a strong enough lobby in domestic politics to ensure that the Government would protect farmers against falls in income brought about by overproduction. For years, the Government took surpluses off farmers' hands, distributing them below cost in either domestic or foreign markets, or storing them. The best known programme of this sort was the Agricultural Trade Development and Assistance Act of 1954, generally known as Public Law 480 (PL 480) or the Food for Peace Programme.

At the domestic level, urban, consumer, welfare, and labour interests advocated public policies for cheap food, while the farmer strove to maintain his income. As the political context changed in the 1960s, the interests of the farm bloc were jeopardized by public pressure against the massive export of surplus food as aid. The Nixon Administration readjusted the situation in favour of the farmers in 1970, and the Senate Agriculture Committee declared in its report on the 1973 farm bill that "we should urge farmers to continue to produce for the world market so that agricultural exports will be increased".[5] Agriculture's new strength in the Nixon era can also be seen in the American approach to trade, particularly in the General

5. Rosenfeld, op. cit. pp. 19-20

Agreement on Tariffs and Trade (GATT) negotiations beginning in September 1973. American officials sought to eliminate those foreign trade barriers which prevented the strong agro-industries from improving the American trade and payments position - a policy of food for cash.

Consequently, commercial food exports rose to $20 billion, while Food for Peace shipments dropped below $1 billion. Food for Peace recipients must have felt the political and psychic costs involved in this process. PL 480 was not primarily a surplus disposal programme, but rather an American national security instrument, only secondarily for humanitarian purposes. Politically, the programme helps infuse purchasing power in countries perceived of as vital to American defence and security. For over three decades American governments have used food as a political tool to relieve the hardship of American friends (sparing them the cost of buying food on the open international market and helping them keep popular discontent within manageable bounds); to show off American productivity and generosity; and to bargain for other benefits.

A guideline to understanding American food policy after the 1973 crisis appears in a statement of the former American Secretary of State, Henry Kissinger, during his Senate confirmation hearings in September 1973, asked whether there had been systematic thinking about the new relationship between agriculture and diplomacy, Kissinger answered: "It is a new field for us. We had not in the past thought that agricultural exports required foreign policy decisions".[6] Asked whether he could initiate discussions with the main

6. Rosenfeld, op. cit., p.17.

exporting nations as to what measures should be taken in the light of the world food supply situation, Kissinger responded:

> We have always resisted the idea of commodity-type agreements because we wanted to have maximum opportunity for the export of American products, and we thought we would have enough to take care of all needs. In this respect the last year (1972-73) has been a challenge to all our traditional assumptions.[7]

The Sudan and Public law 480

On 14 November 1961, after three years of negotiations, the Sudan signed a two year, $4.16 million agricultural commodities agreement with the United States. The agreement was renewed in 1963 and again in 1966. Preliminary discussions about a third renewal, involving agricultural commodities worth $11.55 million, terminated when Sudan broke diplomatic relations with the United States as a result of the 1967 Middle East War.[8] The initial agreement dealt mainly with wheat grain, wheat flour, and rice, but dried milk and tobacco were added in the 1963 renewal, sorghum in the 1966 accord.

The Sudan government had begun corresponding with the American government in January 1959 in the hope of concluding an agreement under which the Sudan would utilise the facilities extended by the American Agricultural Trade Development Act (Public Law 480, or PL 480), as amended in 1954. At the time - just two months after the military regime of General Abboud had come to

---

7. Ibid, p. 26.

8. Ministry of Foreign Affairs, Khartoum. File on American Aid, ID Sheet and pp. 126-155.

power - the Sudan was experiencing an acute shortage of foreign exchange and had no stable arrangements with any other country for the supply of such agricultural commodities as wheat flour, rice, and dried milk. Before the 1958 coup, the Sudan annually imported 5000 metric tons of rice from Egypt, but after some border problems in the Halaieb area of northeastern Sudan supplies from Egypt became less sure This may have been a move by President Nasser to create political difficulties for the infant military government. In any event, the Sudanese difficulty in getting wheat from Egypt itself an underdeveloped country - suggests that it is not only the big powers which use agricultural commodities as levers to influence policy or to indicate disagreements with trade partners. To offset this problem, the Sudan made an agreement with France in 1958 by which it received 50,000 metric tons of wheat flour against cotton deliveries, but the pact was not renewed for 1959. These were the circumstances in which the Sudan sought the assistance of the United States. U.S. officials in Khartoum were eager to conclude an accord, particularly after a Soviet delegation arrived in March to negotiate a Sudanese-Soviet trade agreement.[9] When the Soviet delegation came to terms with the Sudanese, American enthusiasms for a PL 480 agreement temporarily cooled. In the prevailing Cold War atmosphere, the two powers were each trying to win over the military regime, revealing their desire to create spheres of influence in newly independent states.

When U.S. aid to Sudan stopped in 1967 it remained suspended for seven years. Dr F. Machmer, a USAID official at the American Embassy in Khartoum, explained

9. C.B. Molane, Soviet-Third World Relations, Vol. III, 1974, p. 137.

the resumption of American aid to the Sudan in terms of Sudan's attitude towards the Sinai Agreement, the mediation of the Sudanese President in the release of two Americans detained by the Eritrean Liberation Front, and the June 1976 visit by President Nimeiri to the United States. Taken together, these events gave the United States sufficient reason to step up economic cooperation in the fields of agricultural development, educational training, and infrastructure building.[10]

Public Law 480 ("The Agricultural Trade Development And Assistance Act") was enacted by Congress on 10 July 1954, and later amended on 6 September 1958. The amended law has three main points: agicultural commodities may be sold to foreign countries against payment in the recipients' local currency (Title I); they may be donated by the U.S. government to the receiving government for disaster relief (Title II); and they may be donated by the U.S. government to voluntary American people-to-people organisations for free distributions to needy persons overseas (Title III).

Title I of the Act most directly concerned the Sudan, since it allowed for the sale of surplus American commodities at approximate world market prices through normal marketing channels and with payment in the currency of the importing country. The purchase had to be over and above the recipient's normal imports from other friendly countries. Sales from the U.S. were arranged through normal commercial channels and importation could be through the same channels in the importing country or through a purchasing office operating in the United States, either independently or under the

10. Interview with Dr F. Machmer, August, 1976.

embassy of the importing country. There were also specified procedures for payment for the comodities, in local currencies, to the account of the United States government.

PL 480 agreements stipulated that a percentage (of the funds accruing from the sale of surplus agricultural commodities) - usually about 60% - was to be made available to the importing country in the form of long term loans, usually for periods of thirty or forty years and at reasonable interest rates. Payments on these loans could be made in local currency or in dollars, at the option of the borrower. Of the remaining 40% of proceeds, up to 25% was to be available to American business firms and their branches, subsidiaries, or affiliates for investment in projects approved by the importing country; and to local firms which would invest the funds in facilities intended to increase the consumption of American surplus agricultural commodities purchased under PL 480. The balance of the proceeds were used to meet American expenditure in the importing country. These often include embassy expenditure, financing student exchange programmes, and purchasing general supplies and services. In some cases the US Government may make grants from these funds in local currency for financing such projects as roads, clearance of slum residential areas, and irrigation. However, none of the PL 480 account funds can be used without the joint consent of the U.S. government and the borrowing country.

The Politics of Aid: The Sudanese-American Commodities Agreement of 1959 and 1963

Applications for purchase of surplus commodities under PL 480 originate either in Washington with the embassy of the applying country or through the American Ambassador in the country. Joint negotiations then address the following questions: the type and amount of agricultural commodities required as well as the specifications and nutritive qualities that would best meet the preferences and tastes of the consuming population; terms of payment; and purpose for which the U.S. funds accruing from the sale of these commodities are to be spent.

When the government of the Sudan approached the U.S. government in January 1959 concerning PL 480, it was the first time the Sudan had asked for food aid from the United States. The preliminary response was favourable and negotiations were scheduled to begin early in February. The completion of the Soviet-Sudanese trade agreement shortly thereafter, however, irritated the Americans, and while consultations continued for twelve months, they reached a deadlock in late December 1959. The Sudan renewed its application in August 1960, but the characteristically slow paced negotiations consumed another thirteen months before resulting in an agreement for the purchase of $4.6 million worth of food - 36,000 tons of wheat and 20,000 tons of wheat flour.

An examination of similar contemporary agreements helps place the Sudanese case in perspective. In 1958 the United States signed a PL 480 contract with Ireland for $3 million and another with the United Arab Republic for approximately $25 million. A third agreement in 1960 provided for the sale to India of commodities worth more $1.2 billion over a four year period. While these accords were being framed, the Sudan was trying to find acceptable terms for the purchase of only $3.5 million in surplus wheat, wheat flour, and rice. It took the Sudan thirty-four months to obtain this food.

The PL 480 with Iceland allocated 19.5% of the funds for U.S. expenditures; 25% for the Exim Bank; and 55.5% as a loan for Iceland. The Sudan government requested similar treatment regarding the loan element of its agreement, but the request was denied.[11]

The United States' first PL 480 agreement with Egypt in 1958 was limited to wheat, wheat flour and shipping costs only. 75% of the proceeds were used to meet American expenditure in the UAR; the remaining 25% were for Exim Bank expenditures. No part of this money was a gift to Egypt, although the amount assigned to cover U.S. expenditure in the UAR seems too big for embassy expenses. This presents the danger of the donor country using this money for its own political ends within the recipient country. Such funds can also enter the market surreptitiously and inflate the prices of consumer goods.

A second USA-UAR PL 480 followed five months later. The United States Department of Agriculture revealed the agreement with the following official announcement on 5 May 1959:

> The U.S. Department of Agriculture (USDA) today announced commodity details of a supplemental agreement between the United States and the United Arab Republic which provides for financing the sale of $23.4 million worth (including certain ocean transportation costs) of U.S. agricultural commodities for Egyptian pounds. The agreemnnt was negotiated under Title I of the Agricultural Trade Development and Assistance Act of 1954 (Public Law 480, 83rd Congress) as amended.
>
> The comodity composition of the agreement is as follows:

11. Ministry of Foreign Affairs, Khartoum. Letter, 22 June 1959.

	million dollars
Tobacco (approx. 10 million pounds)	9.0
Rice (approx. 880.000 CWT)	5.3
Cotton seed and/or soybean oil (approx. 22 million pounds)	3.2
Yellow corn (approx. 2 million bushels)	2.6
Grain sorghums (approx. 350,000 bushels)	0.4
Barley (approx. 230.000 bushels)	0.3
Frozen Poultry (approx. 1.3 million pounds)	0.5
Nonfat dry milk (approx. 550.000 pounds) Anhydrous milk fat (approx. 770,000 pounds)	0.5
Ocean transportation (estimated)	1.6
Total	23.4

Sales under this programme will be made by private U.S. traders. Details of purchase authorization will be announced.

25% of the Egyptian pounds as sales proceeds will be set aside for loans to U.S. and U.A.R. private enterprise. These loans will be made by the Export-Import Bank of Washington.

Thus, the Sudan was struggling to obtain a single $3.5 million loan while Egypt received two loans in a six month period. The reasons for this were rooted in the international political situation and the cold war mentality of the time. Egypt, though friendly to the USSR, nevertheless commanded assistance from the United States because of its centrality to the issues of Israel and Palestine, its control of the Suez Canal, and its strategic importance to big power politics. The Sudan's poverty, military weakness, and lack of a position geographically strategic to America's foreign policy aim of communist containment meant that it did not command big power interests that warranted supplying aid.

Ethiopia had long been a United States favourite in Africa because of its command of the southern Red Sea and the Straits of Bab al-Handab, and this rendered the Sudan strategically useless. These very circumstances probably impelled the USSR to seek influence in the Sudan between 1956 and 1971 in the hope of counteracting the U.S. presence in Ethiopia. As this approach failed, Soviet interest shifted to southern Yemen and, later, Somalia. When the political situation changed in Ethiopia and Egypt fell more closely in step with the United States the Sudan became eligible for the purchase of American military equipment. The Washington Post of 17 November 1976 said:

> President Ford has taken another significant step to deepen U.S. involvement in Africa by formally declaring that Sudan, the largest country on the continent, is eligible for the purchase of American military equipment.... His declaration.... is a major move in U.S. efforts to encourage Sudan to play a role as a buffer state to the more radical Arab and African states adjoining it.

Clearly, the granting of aid involves many conditions and requirements, at least some of which a recipient country must fulfil before it becomes "eligible". Aid is not necessarily given to the needy to ward off economic problems, but rather to countries that serve the interests of the donor in certain political situations. When eligibility has been established, from the donor's point of view, the signal is given to governmental and para-governmental institutions that aiding a particular country serves the national interest of the donor.

Another country whose aid agreement with the United States under PL 480 is of interest in India in 1960.[12] President Eisenhower and Indian Agricultural Minister S.K. Patel signed an agricultural commodities agreement in Washington on 4 May 1960 by which the United States sold India $1.27 billion in goods, including seventeen million tons of wheat and a million tons of rice, over a four year period.

Fifteen per cent of the total loan was allocated for shipping rice and wheat to India, with the condition that half the total be carried on American vessels. The agreement stipulated that if American shipping costs exceeded those of foreign carriers, the U.S. government would pay the difference. The government of India paid the amounts accruing from these commodities sales (in Indian currency), into a special account in the name of the U.S. government in India. The amount accruing from sales was to be spent as follows:

42% as a grant to the Indian government for economic development projects;

42½% as a loan to the government of India; and

15% on joint projects between the two contracting governments, and on official expenses of the American government within India.

Between 1954 (when PL 480 came into effect) and the signing of this agreement in 1960, India obtained agricultural commodities worth about a billion dollars. This was the largest Pl 480 programme in the world. The 1960 agreement gave India the opportunity to guarantee her wheat and rice needs for the following four years. The accord was signed just five months after President

---

12. Information about this agreement is contained in a report from the Sudanese Ministry of Foreign Affairs (MFA), MFA letter No. 3/A/64, 22 June 1960.

Eisenhower's state visit to India in December 1959 and presents a striking example of the American policy of containment playing a major role in the flow of American money overseas.

In September 1962 the Sudan entered into successful negotiations to extend the time frame of the 1961 agreement. In August, 1965, four months before the termination of the renewed agreement, the Sudan sought again to renew the accord, this time for three years and with a proposed total of $11.5 million. The American Embassy in Khartoum responded negatively to this request, at least in part, turning down a three year renewal on the grounds that current legislation authorrized the negotiation of only a one year agreement.[13] The Sudan had no choice but to accept, and the renewal was signed on 13 April 1966.

The American Embassy also noted that other 1966 legislation effected Pl 480. The law already required that negotiations take into account the grantee's technical agricultural potential and financial resources and its capacity to allocate sales proceeds to a wide range of food production and other projects. The 1966 Food for Peace Act, whose provisions came into effect on 1 January 1967, regulated new sales agreements in foreign currencies, dollars on credit, or foreign currencies on credit convertible into dollars. The law also applied to dollar credit sales to private sector trade entities in recipient countries if they engaged in certain kinds of transactions. Specifically, the legislation empowered the President to:

---

13. Ministry of Foreigh Affairs, Khartoum. Note from U.S. Embassy, Khartoum, No. 742, 31 December 1966.

make sales agreements only with those countries which he determines to be friendly to the United States... As used in this Act "friendly country" shall not include for purposes only of sales of agricultural commodities under title I of this Act, any Nation which sells or furnishes or permits ships or aircrafts under its registry to transport to or from Cuba or North Vietnam (excluding United States installations in Cuba) any equipment materials, or commodities so long as they are governed by a Communist regime: provided, that with respect to furnishing, permitting, or selling, and transporting to Cuba medical supplies, non-strategic raw materials for agriculture of food comodities, sales agreements may be entered into if the President finds with respect to each country and so informs the Senate and the House or Representatives of the reasons therefore, that the making of each such agreement would be in the national interest of the United States and all such findings and reasons therefore shall be published in the Federal Register.[14]

The Terms of the Agricultural Commodities Agreement

A short introduction precedes the articles of the 1961 agricultural commodities agreement. This preamble states the main objective of PL 480 as the expansion of trade in agricultural commodities in a manner which will not disrupt normal trade patterns and prices. This idea is repeated in several later articles of the agreement. Nevertheless, all PL 480 agreements are bound to have some effect on the existing pattern of trade

14. Ministry of Foreign Affairs, Khartoum. Note from U.S. Embassy, Khartoum, No. 26, November 1966.

between the recipient countries and their normal suppliers. For example, the Sudan exported maize to Egypt before the latter signed an agricultural commodities agreement with the United States in December 1958, at which time the trade ceased.[15] This case illustrates why commodity agreements have often aroused objections from suppliers and subjected the American government to the criticism of even its friends and allies. The Sudan objected to the inclusion by the United States of both short and extra long staple cotton in PL 480 agreements, since this disrupted Sudan's cotton trade and affected its markets. PL 480 expressly states the desirability of expanding trade with other countries "in a manner which would not displace usual marketings of the United States in these commodities" but it makes no mention of the "usual marketings" of the importing country. American legislators are primarily concerned with American interests, and it is economic, trade, political, and strategic issues, not the"humanitarian" intentions referred to in the "Food for Peace" Philosophy, which determine the direction and amount of aid.

The first articles of the Sudanese-American Agreement 1961 and that of 1963 are essentially the same, repeating the proposition that the agreement should not unduly disrupt "normal" patterns of American trade. In it, also, the U.S. government undertakes to finance Sudan government purchases of certain American surplus agricultural commodities. The availability of goods for use in PL 480 programmes is determined by seasonal fluctuations, production magnitudes, levels of domestic

15. Ministry of Trade, Khartoum. Letter No. WTCT*/1/1 48/g, 26 September 1962.

American consumption, the state of ordinary trade, and the requirements of other aid projects. The list of available commodities is subject to continuous revision. Under this article, negotiations analyze the quantities required by borrowers, the export market value, and the specifications asked for in each product. Similarly, purchase authorizations, provisions relating to the actual sale and delivery of the commodities, and the deposit of borrowed currency are agreed upon under this article. It further states that purchase must be made from American agricultural commodity markets in the United States by agents of the borrowers and that delivery must be made on United States flag vessels.

Articles III, IV, and V are standard provisions which meet various requirements of the 1954 Act. Of much greater interest is Article II. The provisions of the Second Article of both accords do not differ, although breakdown of percentages of the proceeds does differ. This article deals with Section 104 of the original Act, which concerns uses of the foreign currency accruing to the American Government from sales of the commodities. Section 104 lists fifteen different uses for the borrower's currency accruing from sales. These break down into three distinct categories (strategic, cultural and economic), carefully calculated to serve American domestic pressure group interests and American foreign policy.

With respect to strategic interests, for example, Section 104 outlined the need for recipient countries to "develop" rather than "to purchase or to contract to purchase strategic and critical materials". The latter phase could include anything from cotton to an earth satellite station to a nuclear reactor to the most sophisticated strategic weapons of our age. Another clause dealt with the purchase of American military equipment as one aim of the Act. These issues did not concern the Sudan in the early 1960s; all that it wanted was food. The borrower had no choice, however, but to accept the whole section as legislated or leave the whole agreement.

Those clauses of Section 104 pertaining to "cultural" obligations are less offensive, since financing translation of books, disseminating scientific information, and assisting American schools are minor issues, less directly associated with problems of State sovereignty. Regarding economic matters, however, four subsections of Section 104 emerge as prominent areas of disagreement in many PL 480 negotiations.

The first one allows the use of accumulated funds for "financing the purchase of goods or services for other friendly countries". This enables the United States to buy Sudan's goods for the benefit of another country. The United States may also purchase commodities from a third country on behalf of a fourth country, paying for them with earnings accruing in local Sudanese currency or from Sudan's foreign reserves. This clause works exclusively to the advantage of the United States. During the negotiations of the first agreement the United States required the Sudan to sign a letter of understanding, undertaking to provide facilities for the conversion of $50,000 worth of Sudanese pounds into other currencies. These facilities were needed to finance U.S. government agricultural market development activities in other countries. The Sudanese negotiators persistently opposed this, viewing it as a mechanism to facilitate U.S. trade with third countries.

The Sudan government's initial application for PL 480 aid came because of Sudan's need to rectify a serious balance of payment problem. A stipulation compelling the Sudan to make a substantial amount of convertible currency to the United States defeats the whole purpose of the request. If the agreement intended to relax the balance of payment situation, it could not do so by further draining the country's already meagre foreign reserve. The Sudan would have been giving away foreign currency that it was trying to save to improve its balance of payments. The arrangement was also distateful in that the country into whose currency the United States would request the conversion was not stated in the text. It would be a country friendly to the United States, but would it be friendly to the Sudan? The Sudan did not wish to have its goods sold to an unfriendly country. Moreover, no such provision was included in the agreements signed between the United States and Egypt, Iceland, or India at more or less the same time.

The United States sought another letter of understanding in the early stages of the negotiations of the first agreement. First, it requested the Sudan to submit a statement of its annual import of rice and the Department of Statistics provided the following information:

Year	Sudan's import of rice (in tons)	Price in L.S.
1955	5710	207724
1956	2100	82873
1957	4820	238027

On receipt of these figures, the United States demanded that the Sudan import in 1959, with its own foreign exchange and from free world sources, at least 5000 tons of rice. American sources believed that the volume of Sudan's domestic production that year would be below normal, thus making it an "abnormal" year - one of the indicators which made Sudan eligible for assistance under PL 480. The Sudan responded that such an undertaking would be very difficult, particularly in that the 4000 tons requested for 1959 represented all the rice the country needed for that year.

A second problem area concerned loans administered by the Export-Import Bank of Washington D.C. (Exim-Bank or Exim) as the agent of the U.S. government with the Bank of Sudan as its counterpart. Loans under this sections fall under the PL 480 agreement but are assigned by the American government to the discretion of the Exim-Bank. Funds are made available, with the consent of the Bank of Sudan and Exim-Bank, to either Sudanese or American businessmen for the sole purpose of economic development in the Sudan.

Exim-Bank's involvement imposes several conditions and limitations. First, this part of the loan cannot be used in the production of commodities which will compete with American agricultural commodities. This clause deliberately obstructs the development of particular products in the recipient country, opening the market for American products and giving the United States a guaranteed market for surplus agricultural comodities on behalf of the farm bloc. The law opens new markets for American commodities and then seeks to protect those markets. It does not encourage import substitution projects which may eventually make the borrower independent of American agricultural commodities. In this way American aid carefully fosters American trade and discourages self-reliance, despite its lip service to this concept.

A second limitation prohibits the use of these funds in the public sector. On the other hand, the private sector, and especially American owned private enterprises, are encouraged, as the latter may borrow from these funds to meet local currency needs and expenses. This accords with the conviction that capital breeds capital to reinvest and reproduce itself, thus guaranteeing the capitalist path to "development".

PL 480 established the maximum allocation for the Exim-Bank at 25% of the total proceeds of sales made under the agreement. This provision could benefit the borrower if most of the money took the form of loans to local private enterprises in the receiving country. In the first agricultural commodities agreement with Sudan, the Americans demanded the maximum allocation for the Exim-Bank.

The real problem with this part of the legislation is that it is usually read in conjunction with another key paragraph of the act which gives the Exim-Bank and its successor in the 1966 agreement, USAID, the authority to use Sudanese pounds which have been set aside for loans for any purpose authorized by Section 104 if loans have not been arranged within three years. If appropriately utilized, this too, may help the receiving country since the borrower may relend these sums to local private business for development purposes and the borrower need not pay interest on funds appropriated by the Exim-Bank if they are not used as loans within three years. If a sum accumulated for three years the Exim-Bank has the authority to use the funds for any purpose designated in Section 104. This facilitates the development of the private sector and avoids the accumulation by the United States government of local currencies which could otherwise be used to strengthen the economy of the recipient country.

Another clause of Section 104 which caused some dissatisfaction in the negotiations provided for the use of part of the commodity proceeds to meet U.S. government obligations in the Sudan. These included mainly the expenses of the American Embassy and the U.S. Information Service. No percentages were specified for this purpose, but the accepted practice has been 10% of the remaining 75% of the proceeds.

A final portion of Section 104 concerns loans to the Sudan government for the general economic development of the public sector as opposed to those funds discussed above which focus on private enterprises. This subsection is advantageous to the Sudan since it allocates part of the proceeds to easy term development, with repayment varying between twenty and thirty years. The provision does not specify the amount of the remaining 75% of proceeds which may be used in this way, which is occasionally extended as a grant to the receiving country, although this is not stated in the agreement. If the borrower does not insist on this, or if it fails to present a strong argument, the clause turns to the advantage of the United States which would naturally, prefer to give the whole 75% as a loan.

It would seem, then, that a shrewd and tough negotiator might obtain as much as 85% of the local currency proceeds for the benefit of the recipient country depending, of course, on variables relating to the state of diplomatic and political relations. However, an examination of actual agreements signed with other countries shows that about 60% goes to the U.S. government.

Section I of the Memorandum of Understanding concerns consultations between the two governments on the dates of shipments, which must be fixed as soon as the agreement is signed. Section II specifies the quantities of goods, which were to be inserted after the agreement was finalized. It also required the borrower to state its "normal" commercial imports of these commodities from other sources and to show that the quantities obtained under the agreement represented a consumption demand over and above this "normal" level.

The concept of "normality" is both vague and misleading. The borrower must first determine its average normal needs and then its additional requirements which would have been not from its own foreign exchange under normal conditions. The Americans expect these additional needs to be justified in terms of increased consumption trends, a higher standard of living, a population increase, or the like. Sometimes the United States asks for data on anticipated annual production or actual production in certain years. Although this may be acceptable to some countries, such figures may disclose to the United States information which a recipient may consider secret or clasified. A prospective recipient of American aid may lose the aid if it declines to furnish such information.

The Political Profile of U.S. - Sudanese Aid Relations

The United States started extending grant aid even before Sudan's independence in 1956 and total American aid, including military assistance, between 1946 and 1975 amounted to LS45.3 million ($126 million). Loans represented about 37% of this amount, with grants constituting the remaining 64%. If military assistance is excluded, LS36.7 million ($102 million), or 55%, came as loans while the remaining 45% or LS23 million ($64.5 million), was assistance, 45% in the form of aid, the rest as grants.

Political relations between the Sudan and United States experienced several up-and-downs after 1956. Cordial relations existed during the Abboud regime between 1958 and 1963. The 1964 political upheaval which, in its early phase, was supported by the Soviet Union resulted in a shrinking of American influence and a slowdown in U.S. aid. The Sudan broke diplomatic relations with the United States in June 1967, resuming them only in July 1972. During those five years the Sudan received no aid. In 1969 a coup led by radical allegedly pro-Soviet, officers took place. Sudan established closer relations with the USSR. An article in the American press suggests how unfriendly relations with the U.S. were at the time.

> One of the lunar rocks U.S. astronauts collected on their first trip to the moon... reveals much about the changing relationships between Khartoum and Washington. Those relations were so strained in the 1970s that Sudan refused to accept the ceremonial rock gift (extended by U.S.A.). For months it was kept in the safe of the Netherlands Embassy (maintaining the U.S. interests section) here while American diplomats awaited a thaw in the hostility between the two Governments![15]

The rupture in Sudan-Soviet relations following the July 1971 coup and counter-coup prompted American official circles to react positively to Sudan's call for assistance. The settlement of the southern problem in March 1972 and restoration of diplomatic ties with the

15. Los Angeles Times, Sunday, May 15, 1977.

United States in July - making Sudan the first Arab State to restore relations and earning it considerable resentment from other Arab countries - marked a turn towards a normalization of relations which was abruptly interrupted by the assassination in March 1973 of U.S. Ambassador Cleo Noel and his aide, George Moore, by the Palestinian Black September Group. The uneasy atmosphere following the assassination worsened when the Sudan government released the persons responsible for the attack. In response, Washington recalled its ambassador in protest in June 1974 and the aid process slowed down.

An official U.S. embassy report, dated 15 December 1972, reveals the attitudes of American officials on political and economic development in the Sudan.[16] The report dealt with "economic trends" over an eighteen month period and made several key points. First, it observed that the most notable development in the Sudan's economy during the period surveyed was the "sharp switch in direction by the Government away from an ideologically oriented, nationalistic policy to a more pragmatic attitude with emphasis on a mixed company and a desire to seek help from all sources". By March 1971 the Nimeiri regime had become disillusioned with the results of its earlier policy which "concentrated on ties with the Eastern European bloc and the revolutionary regimes in Libya and Egypt, and at home on socialism in the form of hasty takeovers of both

---

16. The report, written by the late George Moore, Covered the period from July 1971 to December 1972. It was addressed to the Department of State and entitled "Economic Trends Report for the Sudan: an Annual Submission". The report seems to have been released to American businessmen on 17 December - only two days after it had been written.

foreign and Sudanese firms". Aid from the Eastern bloc consisted largely of export credits with the goods involved often expensive and of inferior quality while the Sudanese cotton provided in return was appearing "through the back door" in such traditional markets as India. The nationalized and confiscated enterprises were almost without exception in the red and domestic investment, not to mention the flow of foreign capital, was at a standstill.

With the events of July 1971, the local Communists were discredited. With aid from the Eastern bloc neither desired nor offered, the "Nimeiri Government, both by inclination and necessity, turned to the West and to the private sector, both foreign and domestic". This new policy led to overtures to Western-backed international institutions such as the IMF.

> The World Bank was called upon for assistance. A standby agreement was reached with the IMF which not only provides needed foreign exchange assistance through allocations of Special Drawing Rights (SDRs), but also include a recognition by Sudan that its financial house must be put in order and an agreed plan towards that end devised. At the same time, the IBRD was bringing its influence to bear to compliment the IMF's stabilization efforts and in favour of a revitalized private sector in the country.

In terms of bilateral aid, the report continued, Sudan's major benefactor remained the People's Republic of China which pledged over $80 million for various projects. The aid seemed free of political strings, but the government was also eager for aid from the West. The only major new donor was the Federal Republic of Germany, but the report anticipated a resumed American aid programme "now possible with the resumption of diplomatic relations". Great Britain appeared ready to provide additional help "if some movement can be made on the issue of compensation for the largely British owned nationalized firms" whose takeover, the government now acknowledged, had been a mistake. Official spokesmen had "gone out of their way to express the Government's desire to revitalize the private sector, including attracting both domestic and foreign capital". A new investment law was enacted and Nimeiri declared that all confiscations involving properties owned by Sudanese would be reviewed with the aim of returning these assets where warranted.

The report assessed the implications of the economic scene for the United States in the following terms:

1) U.S. trade and investment were clearly welcomed and desired by the Sudan.
2) U.S. goods and "the American way" were liked and respected in the Sudan. This attitude was deemed unlikely to change in the near future because the country wanted quality items despite foreign exchange problems.
3) U.S. suppliers were at a disadvantage compared with the more traditional markets of Western Europe because of the latter's proximity. However, the shifting world monetary situation made American prices more competitive and suppliers had good opportunities to make inroads. "As external assistance, including USAID, increases, these opportunities lie with the Government and its semi-autonomous agencies. A key factor in trading with the Sudan is the question of credit. U.S. suppliers, with the U.S. Export-

Import Bank once more offering its facilities in the Sudan, are in a much better position than a year ago. But in view of Sudan's debt repayment burden, Exim-Bank will probably look with favour on export-oriented projects generating direct foreign exchange earnings for the United States".

The report continues: "it appears that one of the purposes of the Sudan Government in resuming relations with the United States was to obtain better access to the capital potentially available from U.S. sources for investment purposes. In seeking to attract such capital, the Government appears to be flexible as to the nature of the investment and as to the question of Sudanese participation, whether private or public. Such participation may be a useful selling point, but its absence need not be a stumbling block to a successful proposal". As to the security of such investments, the new investment law was an improvement over its predecessors. More importantly, the report says, "for this government, and quite possibly for its successors, the lessons of the past are not likely to be easily forgotten".

This is how the American Embassy in Khartoum analyzed the political and economic situation in Sudan in 1972. The content of the report explains, to a large extent, why USAID committed $11 million to the long-standing Rahad Irrigation Project in 1973. It also helps to explain why the United States offered Sudan sizeable amounts of American wheat grain in 1973 and in subsequent years. The availability of the report to American businessment at the time of a critical shift in Sudan's foreign policy, accounts for the upward movement in the involvement of American private enterprise in the country and for the pledge of investment in the agricultural field. Joint Sudan-American follow up committees have been formed to report on the progress of projects negotiated both officially and privately. The office of an assistant to the President for Economic Cooperation was created for the first time in 1976, with Dr. Mansour Khalid - an influential figure in the Nimeiri regime - named to it.

Responses of U.S. Aid and Investment Institutions

The improvement of Sudanese-American political and diplomatic relations after July 1971 resulted in a rejuvenation of economic and trade relations. A conference on U.S.-Sudan Trade Development convened in Washington D.C., in March 1973. Over thirty institutions, official and private, and representing a cross-section of American businessmen, investors, and investment guarantors attended the meeting. Official American views were presented by delegates from the Department of State, the Department of Commerce, the Export-Import Bank, the Overseas Private Investment Corporation (OPIC), the Foreign Credit Insurance Association, and the U.S.-Arab Chamber of Commerce.

The Department of State expressed its support of the Sudan's undertaking and noted that the United States was encouraging the expansion of trade and development there. The Department of Commerce also expressed positive views on the development climate in the Sudan, promising to put its resources at the disposal of all interested parties. The Export-Import Bank presented a full range of credit and insurance facilites available to businessmen, most of them in the short-to-medium term range.

The U.S.-Arab Chamber of Commerce, organised to promote and channel trade and investment between the United States and Arab countries, expressed optimism about prospects for trade and development in Sudan based upon several years of experience. Between 1961 and 1967, 500,000 tons of American goods were shipped to the Sudan. The Chamber maintained that the volume of trade in the region, combined with the Sudan's strategic location, offered serious investment possibilities, adding that the Sudan followed a disciplined approach in procurement practices, with all acquisitions based on open competition. The Chamber looked forward to assisting Sudanese and American business efforts in both the private and public sectors.

British Aid

British capital aid to the Sudan from 1956 to 1976 amounted to over LS30 million, or about 5% of the total capital inflow and 7% of total bilateral aid. Almost all British official economic aid to the Sudan took the form of direct bilateral assistance. Three factors account for the relatively small amount of this aid. The first is the diminishing British interest in the region. In the colonial era, the British presence served imperial interests in the Suez Canal, the Red Sea, the Gulf, the Indian Ocean, and the trade routes to Asia. As the British Empire began to disintegrate in the post-war period, British concerns shifted gradually away from the Upper Nile VAlley and the necessity to maintain influence in the area did not exist with the same intensity as before. Secondly, the Sudanese nationalist movement, especially after Egyptian independence in 1922, gained momentum and the 1924 revolution compelled the British to reduce the Egyptian administrative presence and its educational and cultural influence in the Sudan. This, in turn, meant more British expenditures in the Condominium. The 1920s saw the first inflow of British finance capital, termed "Sudan's sinking loans". Finally, for historical reasons, the bulk of British aid has been directed to Commonwealth countries. For example, at the end of 1967 over 11,000 publicly financed British personnel were serving Commonwealth governments.

African countries receive British bilateral economic aid in the form of grants, loans and technical assistance. The Special Commonwealth African Assistance Plan (SCAAD), formed in 1960, administers much of the aid given to Commonwealth countries in Africa. A second aid channel is the Export Credit Guarantee Department (ECGD) and a third is the Commonwealth Development Corporation (CDC), a statuary body in existence since 1948. Initially called the Colonial Development Corporation, it operated only in dependent territories until 1965, when its name changed and it received authorization to operate in Commonwealth countries independent since 1948. In 1969, further alterations empowered the CDC to extend its activities to any developing country, subject to Ministerial approval, and the agency was soon at work, in Ethiopia, Cameroon, Thailand, Indonesia, Zaire, and Tunisia. The objective of the CDC is to invest in projects promoting the economic development of recipient countries. It has undertaken, alone or in association with others, projects in such diverse fields as agriculture, fisheries, forestry, mining, manufacturing, electricity and water supplies, transport, hotels, and property development. CDC sometimes directly owns the projects, but more often its involvement entails loans or equity investments. The projects must yield a return on the capital employed to enable the CDC to service its borrowings. The corporation has no equity capital and depends on loans to finance its investments. With minor exceptions, it obtains these loans from the United Kingdom Exchequer and they are counted against the aid programme. Most British aid to the Sudan has come under the aegis of the ECGD and Ministry of Overseas Development's CDC.

U.K.- Sudan Trade

As the dominant partner in the Condominium, Britain monopolized Sudan's export and import trade before 1956. In its half century of colonial rule Britain did everything possible to make Sudan's economy an export oriented one, dependent on cotton and serving the British textile industry. Britain exported to the Sudan those goods deemed sufficient for her purposes, including industrial products, chemicals, alcohol, and building materials.

After independence, and especially during the first five years of the Ten Year Plan, the value of trade with Britain declined and such new customers as Germany, Italy, India, Japan, the USSR, and China became key trading partners, although the United Kingdom remained first place in the Sudan's import trade. The volume of imports from British sources consistently exceeded Sudan's exports between 1961 and 1969. Exports from Britain increased from LS22 million in 1961 to LS26 million in 1962 to a high of LS27 million in 1963. The average of imports between 1961 and 1969 stood at some LS20 million per year. Average exports and re-exports to Britain during the same period reached only LS10 million, leaving an annual average deficit balance of trade deficit of LS12 million. Despite the sharp decline in Sudan's trade with Britain early in the Ten Year Plan, the country never ceased to request British financial and technical assistance to help implement its development programmes in the 1960s.

Capital Aid

After independence the Sudan signed its first credit agreement with Britain in 1959, with a second one following in 1963.[17] The loans involved LS5 million cash and were channelled through the Export Credit Guarantee Department (ECGD). The first loan was repaid in six semi-annual instalments, with a two year grace period, beginning in mid-1961. The 1963 loan was repayable in twenty years, with an initial five year grace period. The credit purpose of the 1963 credit agreement was to assist the financing of the Ten Year Plan by facilitating the purchase from Britain of equipment needed for the public sector, particularly railway equipment, including rolling stock and heavy accessories; road making equipment; equipment for water and electricity expansion schemes, and diesel locomotives. The loan, executed by the Export Credits Guarantee Department on behalf of the British government, could be used any time within five years of the effective date of the agreement. Repayment was to be in sterling at the interest rate currently applied by the United Kingdom treasury to promisory notes, plus one quarter of one per cent per annum.

At the request of the government of the Sudan at the time of President Ibrahim Abboud's official visit to the United Kingdom in July 1964, the British government offered the Sudan the following financial and technical assistance:

(1) A loan of LS5 million repayable over a period of twenty years, with a five year grace period, and interest charged at the standard current rates

---

17. Ministry of Foreign Affairs, Khartoum. File No. (9) Britain.

for loans of this sort. A press release issued in London during Abboud's visit mentioned that the loan was made in realization of Sudan's financial difficulties and that it represented a further British contribution to the second half of the Ten Year Plan.

(2) Twenty post-graduate scholarships for the academic year 1964-65, in addition to existing training awards and programmes which amounted to LS29,000 as of 1964.

(3) Assistance to improve salaries offered British expatriates for certain government posts in which the salary scale was not sufficient to attract the particular individuals whom the Sudan government wanted.

(4) Aid for the development of Khartoum Technical Institute, including equipment and teaching staff.

(5) The provision, for five years, of scholarships for twenty-five Sudanese teachers of English to undertake one year's training in Britain.

In 1968 the Overseas Development Administration took charge of all British aid previously administrated by ECCD. In the same year, the Sudan government requested aid for the purchase of ten diesel electric locomotives from the English Electric Company and an agreement was concluded in August 1969. It provided an interest free loan of L200,000 for Sudan Railways Corporation for a down payment of 20% of the contract value of the ten locomotives. The loan was repayable over twenty-five years, with a full grace period of two years from the date of signature and a "graduated grace", with an increasing schedule of repayments, for a further five years. Thereafter annual repayments would be in equal amounts until the final instalment. The remainder of the costs of the locomotives was to be financed through a normal Export Credit Guarantee Department credit whose terms stipulated a 20% down payment on placing the order, with the balance repayable in twenty equal semi-annual instalments, the first due six months after the shipment of each locomotive. The interest rate on the credit was 5½% on all outstanding monies, payable at the same time as the semi-annual instalments. In the preparation of the 1970/71 -1974/75 Five Year Plan, it was found that there was an available uncommitted loan balance, which was allotted to projects in the new plan.

In January 1968 the Sudan asked the British government to support a project for replacing forty sluice gates in Sennar dam and making emergency repairs to others. The scheme was agreed to in April 1969 and L459,000 was earmarked as the foreign currency component needed to renovate the dam. The loan was interest free, had a two year grace period, and was repayable in thirteen years, starting in October 1971.

Within six months of the failure of the July 1971 Communist-led coup attempt another loan - the second since Ja'ffer Nimeiri had seized power - was concluded. Under this agreement, Britain extended to the Sudan government an interest free loan of L1,100,000 to help cover the costs of four pumping stations and ancillary equipment needed for the first phase of the Northern Province pump schemes project, a calibrating unit for the Ministry of Irrigation and Hydro-Electric Power, and a visual approach slope indicator for Khartoum Airport. The loan required the exclusive purchase of goods produced in Britain. It allowed a two year grace period, with repayments extending over another twenty-three yeary.

Pump Irrigation Projects in the Northern Province

This project was born in the wake of the 1959 Nile Waters Agreement between the Sudan and the U.A.R., which entitled Sudan to draw additional water from the river. A major aspect of the plan centred around opening new pump schemes on the main Nile and enlarging existing ones. British consultants, carrying out feasibility studies on an area of 165,000 feddans, recommended 32% (52,500 feddans) for pump irrigation development. This area comprised extensions and new schemes at fifteen different sites along the main Nile in the Shendi and Dongola reaches. The total cost of the project was estimated at LS6.3 million, with foreign sources accounting for LS3.53 million. Sudan approached the British government, which responded favourably and dispatched an appraisal mission in April 1969.

The mission, however, recommended the implementation of only three or four schemes in the first stage and advised the United Kingdom to contribute only LS2 million for pumps and pump houses. The Sudan government disliked this offer for several reasons. If the proposed three or four schemes were selected on economic merit, the other ones would not attract foreign capital, since they were essentially subsistence level schemes. To make the selection on any other basis, however, would cause political problems. The latter argument reflects the extent to which the government of the time feared any political repercussions in the area of the proposed schemes or in the capital, where the opposition would lose no chance to portray such incidents as failures of the government to promote rural development. Finally, the British wanted the project spread over four years while the Sudanese believed it could be completed within two.

The Sudanese negotiators worried that the British inclination to choose only the most economically feasible schemes would split the project and add to its total costs, as well as making it difficult to attract other financiers. They concluded that, while the United Kingdom indicated an interest in assisting the Sudan, it had not backed its words with sufficient funds since the downfall of the Abboud military regime. Indeed, in the period from October 1964 to April 1969, Britain never gave a loan of over L2 million in a single agreement, whereas the 1959 and 1963 loans had been worth L5 million each. A partial explanation for the decline lies in political circumstances outside the Sudan. Sudanese-British relations were severed twice between 1964 and 1969 - in December 1965 as a result of the Rhodesian unilateral declaration of independence and again in 1967 after the Arab-Israeli war.

Despite the mission's recommendations, the Sudan government persisted and a formula was finally agreed upon under which the British agreed to give assistance for developing fourteen separate irrigation projects on the main Nile. The plan included a loan of up to L980,000 for phase I of the project, to be used to pay for the pumping plant, the pump stations, and other items which could be purchased from Britain. The loan was interest free and repayable over twenty-five years, with a two year grace period. During the first five years payments were graduated and were administered by the Overseas Development Ministry. The British government also agreed to consider providing loans for phases II and III, subject to the availability of

British funds, the progress of Phase I, and the holding of further discussions with the government of the Sudan.

The implication of these conditions was a British desire to assure flexibility in further negotiations in case of any unforeseen changes of government. This was the first British aid after the 1969 coup d'etat, and it came at a time when most Western countries were withholding aid from what they perceived as a Communist led regime, preferring to "let the dust settle" in Khartoum before making any firm committment of larger aid.

Sudan-United Kingdom Capital Aid and Technical Assistance Programme, 1973-74

In the fiscal year 1973-74, Sudan reached its first agreement with the United Kingdom on a "long term"[18] aid strategy. The programme involved capital aid totalling L11.7 million, which included the unexpended amounts of the 1972 and 1973 loan agreements. It authorized the expenditure of up to L360,000 for replacing sluice gates on Sennar dam and installing ancilliary equipment. Other capital aid and technical assistance contained in the programme included:

Northern Province pump scheme	L 2.5 million
Sennar dam	0.4 "
Cotton storage	0.75 "
Agricultural developmet schemes in southern Sudan	1.5 "
Grain storage	0.35 "
Tea	0.75 "
Generator for Juba	0.2 "
Other Projects	1.2 "
Transportation Projects	4.0 "
	£11.65 million

18. The programme covered only four years but was referred to as "long term" to convey the idea of ongoing British interest in Sudan's development.

The salient features of the capital aid programme were:

(1) The continued, phased, development of the Northern Province pump schemes. The first phase had been part of the 1972 U.K.-Sudan agreement and had included pump schemes at Kitiab, Kelly, El Golid, Geweir, Saiyal, and Sarb Taybia. Phase II was to include projects at A'liab, Mutmir, Wad Hamid, 'Affat, Kabushiya, and Kora. It was expected that both would be complete within four years, at a cost of about L2.5 million.

(2) The execution, subject to economic viability, of a cotton storage project.

(3) Consideration of agricultural projects in the Nuba Mountains, Jebel Marra, South Darfur, and the Red Sea Hills.

(4) A study of mechanization proposals in the Northern Provinces and of modernization and electrification of the Blue and White Nile irrigation projects.

(5) The provision of two generators at Juba and appraisals of grain storage proposals for Aweil, Wau, Renk, Malakal and Juba; and of a tea growing project in the southern region.

(6) A substantial allocation for road development where there was basic evidence of economic viability.

Technical assistance provided assistants for the Academy of Administrative Services and Management Service Units; language training for teachers of English; training for Sudanese nationals in the United Kingdom; the creation and management of a hydraulic research station; and training in electricity management. An important technical assistance proposal by the British government involved establishing a British technical assistance team in Juba, to be composed of four men - an engineer, agriculturalist, animal health and husbandry advisor, and an English language expert.

This particular proposal raised Sudanese suspicions about British intentions. Coming less than two years after the Addis Abbaba Accord for regional self-government, the government was still highly sensitive to issues concerning the south. It was determined to see the accord yield positive results and bring real peace, but feared that such a proposal might have negative results. After several rounds of negotiations, the Sudan refused to accept the proposal.[19] Maintaining political stability in the southern region required the implementation of economic development unhampered by the bureaucratic red tape which usually characterizes aid programmes. Furthermore, in view of Britain's past policy in the south, there seemed every reason to exclude British officials from the south, lest they be agents of British intelligence.

After reaching agreement an aid package of L10,240,000 on capital aid and technical assistance for 1973-77, arranged in 1973. 40% was provided as a grant, 60% as an interest free loan. The grace period was seven and a half years and the loan was to be recovered in seventeen and a half years, making a twenty-five redemption period. Items acquired through the fund had to be purchased in the United Kingdom, as well as being produced or manufactured there.

Attitudes about British aid vary greatly. The countless official efforts to secure development aid illustrate that it has been government policy to accept foreign aid. Sudanese officials sometimes complained about

---

19. Ministry of Foreign Affairs, Khartoum. File No. 9, page 87.

the small size of British aid claimed more British aid on the grounds of Britain's moral obligation to assist the development of a country that it had earlier kept backward and poor. Another argument holds that because British aid is tied to specific projects and limits purchases to British made industrial commodities, it does not really help the Sudan overcome its balance of payments problem. This assertion holds true for all aid from Western countries and confirms the proposition that aid is not charity, but is always given to serve the political and economic interests of the donor. The recipients may either take it or leave it, but cannot forget that there are strings. One cannot assume a moral world in the field of international relations.

AMERICAN AID TO THE SUDAN

THE FIRST DECADE OF AMERICAN AID

By
Salah Khogali

During a lengthy debate in the Sudanese Parliament in the spring of 1958 on the danger of accepting foreign aid in general and American aid in particular, the Umma Party, under the leadership of Brigadier Abdalla Bey Khalil, worked vigorously to secure the passage of a bill allowing American aid. One reason for their success was the weakened state of the Sudanese economy as a result of war in the south.

The aid agreement, signed 16 May 1958, met with criticism not only from the opposition, but also from the press, which observed that "by accepting American aid we exchange British colonizers for American colonizers".[1] "What a black future we are making by accepting U.S. aid",[2] remarked another paper, while a third urged Sudanese to "die with hunger, but not hand over our country to America".[3] Nevertheless, the implementation of the agreement, which included economic and technical aid but had no military aspects, commenced early in the Abboud regime, which came to power in November 1958.

Was it necessary for the military government, which saw itself as revolutionary, to accept American aid in view of the fierce criticisms of Parliament and most of the press, except for El-Neel and El-Umma, which were the papers of the ruling party? In response to this question, Sayed A. Magid Ahmed, who served as

---

1. El Rai Elaam, June 5, 1958.
2. El Ayam, July 3, 1958.
3. El Zumman, August 6, 1958.

Minister of Economics during the first four years of the Abboud government, observed that when the army took control in 1959 the country's finances were so desperate that the government could find no way to start any developmental projects, or even to establish a reasonable balance of payments, without the American aid accord already approved in Parliament.

As to whether the volume of aid was reasonable in light of American contributions to other African countries, Sayed A. Magid pointed out that the amount of aid depended on the policies of both the granting and recipient countries. In this case, American anti-communism harmonized with the the Sudan's official attitudes and helped to explain why, until the end of the Abboud period, the Sudan received a quite reasonable sum.

Between 1959 and 1967 American aid to the Sudan totalled $106,066,970, allocated as follows:[4]

Developmental projects	$64,196,997
Foreign loans	5,000,000
Drainage system loans	2,000,000
Machines for highway and airport maintenance	5,100,000
American textile mill	10,000,000
Wheat and flour agreements	18,770,000

Table 1 outlines some of the terms and conditions of the early loans:

4. Ministry of Finance, U.S.A. Aid and Loans to the Sudan, File No.1, pp. 36-40.

Table 1: V. S. aid 1959-67: terms and conditions

Loan	Conditions
Khartoum North drainage system:	Payable in forty years at 3/4% interest in the first ten years and thereafter 2 1/2%
Maintenance machines for roads and airports:	Payable in forty years at 1% interest in the first ten years and 2 1/2% thereafter.
Industrial Bank:	Payable in forty years at 1% interest in the first ten years, and 2 1/2% thereafter.
Wheat and flour loan:	Payable in thirty-four years at 6 to 7% interest.

Examples of the utility of American aid projects

A few concrete examples of projects financed by American aid from 1959 to 1964 illustrate the importance of this arrangement.

Khartoum-Medani Highway

The Gezira scheme, with its diversified agricultural policy, is unquestionably the backbone of the Sudanese economy. Before the construction of the Khartoum-Medani highway, the trip from the capital to the main city of the Gezira took seven hours during the dry season and more than twelve during the rainy season. Now the trip may be made in three hours at any time of the year.

In 1962 the Sudanese government and the United States Agency for International Development reached

5. This information comes from Ibid, pp. 90-93, and and the American Embassy, Khartoum.

agreement on a project to construct a road linking Khartoum, where most of the oilmills were located, with the Gezira, where ginning factories produced cotton seed. The length of the highway was 186 kilometers, of which 98 kilometers were completed, before the termination of American aid, at a cost of $31,844,921. The remaining 88 kilometers were finished with Sudanese money and expertise in 1969. The highway has played a very significant role in the socio-economic development of villages along its route, as well as in the development of Gezira province as a whole.

Agricultural Aid under PL 480, 1961-67.

From 1961 to 1967, USAID and the Sudan signed five agreements to supply wheat, flour, and other agricultural commodities to the Sudan under the terms of Public Law 480 (the Food for Peace Act). Three of the five agreements came after 1964 and the overthrow of the Abboud regime by a socialist revolution. Several parties, other than the Umma, signed aid agreements with the United States, suggesting that all Sudanese governments, including the communist one of October 1964, agreed upon the need for this kind of aid. Table 2 shows the details of these agreements.[6]

The industrial bank loan

This was one ot the most important loans which the Sudan received from the United States. The LS.2 million involved enabled the bank to give financial assistance to many small industries and also helped to achieve self-sufficiency in such products as soap, food oil, sweet biscuits, and shoes. AID technical advisors assigned to the Industrial Bank oversaw the creation of

6. Ibid., p.49.

Table 2: Aid agreements with United States

Agreement	Commodity	Quantity in Metric tons	Value in $	Public Sector Loans	Private Sector Loans	AID and American Embassy Salaries
One	Wheat & flour	51,179	4,300,000	35%	15%	25%
Two	" " "	66,025	5,600,000	35%	15%	25%
Three	" " "	1,487,490	12,000,000	35%	15%	15%
Four	" " "	56,000	4,160,000	75%	05%	20%
Five	Dura	2,000,000	11,000,000	75%	05%	20%
	Tobacco	200	450,000			

a well-trained staff which later took responsibility for studying proposals for bank loans, recommending those to be accepted and explaining why others were to be rejected. The Industrial Bank is now considered one of the most efficient banks in the country.

A Year of Aid

Before attempting an overall evaluation of American aid to the Sudan, a review of a single year's program will reveal the worth of this aid to the Sudan. In 1967-1968 the approved aid budget was $8,282,383, distributed to a host of Sudanese agencies. The pilot survey of the Khartoum Port Sudan highway conducted by American and Sudanese engineers with American funds, was an important achievement during the year. An important aspect of the 1967-1968 AID plan was an extensive training program. According to American Embassy files, 138 Sudanese from different fields of specialization received training in the United States and in Beirut, Lebanon, at a cost of $348,620.[7] A breakdown of the studies they pursued is given in Table 3.

Table 3: U.S. Aid financed training for Sudanese 1967-68

type of studies	number of officials or technicians.
Agriculture	28
Technical Education	10
Education	29
Industry	6
Transport	14
Economic and Finance	13
Others	4
Sent to Lebanon for Specialized Training	34
Total	138

7. Ministry of Finance, U.S.A. Aid to the Sudan, Training File, 1958, p.48.

Conversely, a considerable number of American experts in many fields provided advice and assisted in planning. Seven worked in agricultural projects; eleven in public works; fifteen in education; twenty-six in the Survey Department; 10 at the Industrial Bank; and 10 for the Lockheed Foundation.[8]

American support of Israel during and after the 1967 war prompted the Sudanese government to break diplomatic relations with the United States. As a result, AID activities ceased and many important projects were delayed or even cancelled if the Sudanese government was unable to finance them.

Aid Evaluation

In assessing American aid between 1959 and 1967, it is worth noting that President Abboud has been the only Sudanese leader able to bring large sums of aid to the country from the United States and the Soviet Union simultaneously. During his regime the country received substantial military aid from the Soviet Union and other socialist countries. Abboud was tactful and shrewd in soliciting aid from both great powers. In fact, the President paid official visits to the United States and the Soviet Union in a single trip and was well received in both capitals. The Americans, who always wanted to excel in the competition thus established, gave the Sudan greater sums than might otherwise have been the case.

During the Abboud years almost 2000 Sudanese received training in the United States. Many of these individuals later led development schemes and some have assumed key government posts. American aid, as previously

---

8. Ministry of Finance, U.S.A. Aid to the Sudan, Experts File, 1978, p.23.

noted, contributed to the construction of what was, at the time, the longest paved road in the country, as well as facilitating the pilot survey for the Port Sudan-Khartoum highway.

AID support for the Industrial Bank immeasurably helped Sudanese industries, but it was in agriculture that AID made its most significant contribution through agricultural extension projects and the establishment of audio-visual aid centres. The Kuko Research Centre, the main poultry research centre in the country, benifited from American funds and financial and technical aid was also given to the large agriculture research stations at Medani and Hodaba.

In the areas of health and education, four new hospitals and many new sections within older ones were financed by the United States, while many doctors were sent abroad for training. The University of Khartoum Faculty of Medicine also received financial help. Secondary schools, technical institutes, and vocational training centres were established; 250 teachers were trained; and a large audio-visual centre established in the Ministry of Education's headquarters, all under AID auspices.

U.S. AID to Sudan after May 1969

Sudan received no American aid in the first five years after Gaafar Nimeiri came to power in May 1969, primarily because of the strong Communist influence in the country until 1971 and uncertainty about the regime's future for the next several years. Although diplomatic relations were restored in 1972, the United States sponsored only two projects of note before 1976, an $11 million loan for the Rahad Scheme and a $3 million loan under Pl 480. President Nimeiri's visit to the

United States in June 1976 led to more regular political relations between the two countries, as well as an upsurge in economic assistance.

A serious difficulty of the present government stems from its tendency to become involved in many developmental projects at one time, while its balance of payments has remained a problem. The balance of payments crisis has serious implications for economic growth and there is evidence that shortages of essential items may hinder Sudan's capacity to produce and market agricultural and livestock products.

By the late 1970s, USAID was contributing to at least twenty-five projects, including Blue Nile Agriculture Development, Western Sudan Agriculture Research, Southern Sudan Manpower Development, Abyei Integrated Rural Development, Rural Planning, the University of Gezira, Darfur Agriculture Production and Degradation, and Western Sudan Agriculture Extension.

The Blue Nile Agriculture Development

The agricultural sector in Sudan provides a livelihood for about 85% of the population, 40% of the grass domestic product, and 95% of export earnings, while utilizing less than 20% of the country's arable land. Almost 90% of the total agricultural output comes from traditional farming on rainfed lands, which helps account for the low level of productivity per farm family and land unit. This project works through the local governments of selected villages in a specific area of the Blue Nile province.

The Sudan Government, IDA, and AID shared the cost of the project over its six year life. AID contributions defrayed the costs of technical advisors, researchers, long and short term training abroad, operating costs, equipment and furniture, vehicles and farm machinery, and a share of operating expenses. The project focused on the four western Sudanese provinces of North and South Darfur and North and South Kordofan, an area of about 850,000 square kilometers with about 5 million people, or some 30% of the country's population. Because of human and livestock population pressures, more and more pastoralists in areas where annual rainfall exceeds 400 mm have turned to production in association with livestock, thus reducing the land available per family. Range areas once seasonally rested during cyclical migrations became subject to intense degradation.

Southern Manpower Development

This is one of the most important projects of AID in the south. Its goal is to strengthen the human resource base in the southern Sudan by training agriculture personnel to work with small farmers.

The development of the southern region suffered badly as a result of the long civil war from 1956 to 1972. The almost total breakdown of educational services was perhaps the most damaging effect of the war and greatly delayed the emergence of a skilled and trained human resource base. Realizing that such a base was imperative for any developmental activity, the southern regional government defined the lack of skilled manpower as the most serious bottleneck in the achievement of its agricultural development plan.

This particular project sought to improve the southern regional government's ability to maintain the rural population, provide basic public services, and improve the cash economy of the area. The southern region is larger than Kenya and has a population of some 4.5 million. The civil war left the road network in a state of complete disrepair, while the regional ministry responsible for it lacked qualified technicians, equipment, and funds. The efficiency of government in delivering services to the rural population; the prospects of solving the very difficult supply situation; the development of agriculture, animal husbandry, and auxiliary economic activities; and the success of the national integration policy all depend on the ability of the southern regional Ministry of Communications, Transport and Roads to maintain a usable network of rural roads.

The Wau-Juba link was designed to generate substantial economic benefits, since Wau is the terminus of the railroad from Khartoum. The plan to rehabilitate the Rumbek-Shambe road had as its goal facilitating the delivery of services to the rural population in this depressed area as well as stimulating the economy by providing an all weather link to the Jonglei canal which, itself, will open a commercial water link between Khartoum and Juba.

American Activities in the Health Field

American aid to the health sector has been intended to alleviate the financial burden borne by the government's extension of a primary health care programme throughout the country. Communicable diseases rooted in poor mainly sanitation comprise the principle health problem of the Sudan and absorb the bulk of its public health resources. Other avoidable diseases consume the next largest amount of health sector funds. Malaria is the single most prevalent communicable disease, afflicting upwards of a quarter of the population. In the Gezira, Sudan's most capital intensive agricultural area, the malaria prevalence rate among children increased from 3% in 1962 to 20% in 1977.

These conditions constitute an obvious drain on productivity, output, and development, and the country's development plans have recognized this. The public health share of the national budget during the late 1970s increased at an average of almost 20% for capital investment, while recurrent expeditures grew at an average rate of 9%. Even allowing for inflation this has greatly increased the availability of health services. In the same time period Sudan increased the total number of hospitals and health centres by 50%, the number of hospital beds by 13%, the number of dispensaries by about 20% and the number of dressing stations by nearly 70%. Most attention concentrated on curative services. The Third Development Plan placed greater emphasis on preventative measures, including immunization and publicity on sanitation and personal hygiene, and on efforts to strike a more equitable balance of health resources allocation.

USAID supports two major health projects in the southern and western Sudan. The Health Sector Support Grant, by providing foreign exchange and local currency resources, fosters a more effective implementation of primary health care projects as well as insuring the availability of financial resources for the general expansion of health facilities throughout the country. The Sudan government intends to construct, equip, staff, or upgrade 2688 primary health care units by 1984, thirty-five of them built with American contributions.

In view of the importance of this program and of USAID'S mandate to bring basic services to the poor, a $35 million American contribution provided Sudan with sufficient foreign exchange to avoid shortfalls of medical equipment, supplies, and instructional materials.

Support for Education

The purpose of the AID education sector grant is to assist in the initiation and operation of multifaceted, multipurpose community oriented programs linked to Sudan's three universities but focusing on villages and towns in remote parts of the country. The grant provides foreign exchange and local currency resources to develop the institutional framework needed to launch such programmes. The programme initially concentrated on Gezira and Juba Universities, but eventually included to rely as heavily on the grant's resources and had less direct contact with the target communities.

The programmes envisioned revolve around establishing and running extramural activities sponsored by all major departments and units of the University. These were to include the promotion of cottage industries, training farmers, studying and analyzing the social environment,exchanging information with similar institutions at home and abroad, and dealing with community health problems. To avoid conflicting or duplicative efforts and insure optimum coverage, careful coordination with local leaders, local governmental bodies, and central government officials is essential. Some of the grant funds were earmarked for the targeted villages and communities, as seed money or revolving loans, to allow them to act upon their new skills and knowledge with programmes of their own. The project should raise, at least incrementally, the standard of living in the communities involved, but its success depends on a well integrated approach, as well as the proper facilities, qualified personnel, and technical support of the quality which institutions of higher learning can provide. It also requires continuous technical backstopping from relevant government and private sector programmes focus on problem solving, particularly attempting to bridge the gap between technology and its adaptation, adoption, and application. Some have contributed substantially to correcting problem situations caused by disease, malnutrition, inadequate housing, poor education, and unemployment or employment only at poverty levels.

The American Assessment

The United States Congress has gone on record as believing that the aid program in the Sudan can serve as a general model for rural development programs in many other places. The House Committee on International Relations stressed the importance of improving the quality of life and raising the income of people in the poor rural areas of western and southern Sudan. Its report urges the creation of relatively self-sufficient regional economies through the integration of four activities:

1) Antidesertification measures, including the establishment of permanent land tenure where appropriate;
2) region by region reconstitution of credit and marketing systems based on the cooperative efforts of producers, government authorities, and others;
3) improvement in agricultural information systems for traditional agriculture, with an emphasis on participation by small farmers and on appropriate technology;
and
4) improvement in the local health environment.[9]

9. Congressional Committee on International Relations Report, H.R. 6714, 1978.

CONCLUSION

There can be no doubt that any country's foreign policy objectives are concrete formulations derived by weighing national interests, the prevailing international situation, and the power available to the state. The United States, as one of the two major world powers, has carefully planned foreign policy objectives, some of which may be achieved through aid grants. The postwar period saw the implementation of several programs of American assistance, including the Marshall Plan for the rebuilding of Western Europe, the Truman Doctrine to provide military and economic assistance to states threatened by Communism, and the Mutual Security Programme to strengthen the defenses of the North Atlantic Treaty Organization (NATO) in Western Europe. The success of the Marshal Plan encouraged American policy makers to utilize foreign aid as a tactical means of combatting instability and thwarting Communist aims in developing countries. By 1952, the Plan had sparked a general recovery in Europe marked by an increase in production levels. The Marshall Plan's efforts to integrate the European economies did not result in a single common market for western Europe, although they did contribute to the formation of the European Economic Community (EEC) and the European Free Trade Association (EFTA).

The United States recognized, in the Food for Peace Program, that the world population explosion has made food supply a matter of increasing importance in international politics. Under that programme surplus agricultural products are sold through regular trade channels for local currency, which the United States then uses to expand international trade, encourage economic development, try strategic materials, pay foreign obligations, promote educational and cultural exchanges, build collective strength, and foster American foreign policy.

The current politics of American aid in the developing countries differs from what it was in the 1950s and 1960s in two important ways. Aid is no longer a series of helpful, but unrelated, projects in a given country. Instead it is a "country programme" both in the sense that host country officials have helped formulate it and that it has priority goals, tailored to the country's needs, to which all the various activities relate. A second major difference is that aid entails a larger measure of non-American involvement. Formerly, "self help" merely meant that the host country was expected to contribute something - labour, money, or materials to each project. This concept has now come to include the host country's making major policy decisions, enacting legislation, and taking administrative action.

American aid to Africa raised the problem of the proliferation of aid programmes. The United States had welcomed the independence of the African countries, but looked askance at the prospect of the continent's becoming excessively dependent on American aid. The United States also hoped, at least prior to the 1961 Congo Crisis, that Africa might be kept out of the Cold War and that the Europeans might address problems as they arose. Most American undertakings in Africa during the 1960s were, therefore, quite small and were candidly referred to as "Presence Programs". Some Americans, including top officials in the African Affairs Section of the State Department, felt that the United States should promote larger scale efforts and an "Alliance for Progress" to help developing African states.

The Sudan may be viewed as a special aid case among African countries in that Soviet involvement in Egyptian affairs during the early Nasser years prompted the United States to make a quick move towards the Sudan as a counter measure. Despite the short term of this early American aid (eight years, largely coinciding with Abboud era), Sudan received about $107,000,000, which greatly helped the socio-economic development of the country. More recently, as Communist influence grew in Ethiopia, Libya, Angola, and South Yemen, the Sudan's attractiveness to the United States again increased. In addition to this external situation, the deterioration of relations between the Sudan and the Soviet Union following the abortive communist inspired coup in 1971 presented the United States with another opening.

In a visit to the United States in September 1978, President Nimeiri gave an excellent description of Sudanese-American relations:

> Our relation today is the most effective defence against the undesireable influences in the area, and the most effective way of promoting peace, solidarity, and human dignity.

SUDANESE-EGYPTIAN RELATIONS 1953-1964

By
Omer Mohamed Ali Mohamed

The histories of Egypt and the Sudan have been linked, largely through their sharing of the Nile, since ancient times. The political, economic, and cultural ties between the two countries are, as a result, unique, and defy comparison with those between any other two countries. In general, the flow of influence has been from north to south, from Egypt to the Sudan. Each country has attempted to dominate the other, but Egypt has had greater success in this endeavour than the Sudan, owing in part to its earlier Arabization and Islamization. Despite these connections, the Sudan has remained quite distinct from Egypt. It is less Arabized, less Islamized, and less developed. These realities have found echoes in the attitudes of the two countries towards each other. Until 1952 Egyptian policy makers believed that the total annexation of the Sudan was the only effective means of safeguarding their interests. They expressed this conviction in calls for the unity of the Nile valley and, accordingly, classified Sudanese nationalists either as unionists (pro-Egyptian) or separatists (anti-Egyptian). They viewed Nile Valley unity as a strategy for influencing conditions in both Africa and the Middle East and for giving both countries, but particularly Egypt, a special position in the Afro-Asian bloc.

Following the Egyptian revolution in 1952, however, a new approach developed. Its most crucial element was the recognition of the Sudan's right to self-determination. In 1953, Egypt and Britain, the co-domini, granted self-government to the Sudanese, who were then asked to opt either for unity with Egypt or independence from both of the condominium powers.[1] From 1953 to 1955 Egypt continued to support the Sudanese unionists and to attempt to undermine British influence in the hope of promoting unity. Despite these efforts, the Sudan became an independent country on 1 January 1956.

In a speech to the Egyptian Advocates' Association in 1977, Fouad Sirag El-Din, the Secretary-General of the dissolved Wafd Party, accused the regime of the July revolution of attempting to separate the Sudan from Egypt by endorsing the principle of self-determination:

> We (the Wafd) had insisted on the complete and total unity between the two parts of the Nile Valley. The majority of our Sudanese brothers had supported this opinion".
> "After 1952 the situation changed: Egypt and the Sudan became two independent countries ... We do not wish to deny happiness to our Sudanese brothers or independence if it is their wish".[2]

---

1. An Egyptian scholar places the motivation for this decision on Egypt's desire to terminate British influence in the Sudan. "Even if complete independence were chosen, once Britain evacuated the Sudan, it would be free of foreign influence that could threaten the Nile. Also, once the evacuation was achieved, Egypt could always exercise influence through other means and even force its influence if the necessity should arise". See Tareq Y. Ismael, The UAR in Africa: Egypt's Foreign Policy under Nasser (Evanston, 1971), p. 17.

2. Sirag El-Din, Fouad: Li Maza al-Hizb al-Guned, 1977, pp. 64-65.
The Arabic text was as follows:

لكن نحن قد أهملنا فى هذا السبيل ـ ونحن لم نحرص على
هذه الوحدة بعد ١٩٥٢، حرصنا عليها قبل ١٩٥٢!! ولذلك
كانت النتيجة (الانفصال) ـ وأرجو أن تعود الوحدة الكاملة
الشاملة كما كانت.

Egyptian nationalist leaders had never accepted the strong British presence in the Sudan which the 1899 condominium agreement had established. They justified their demands for the unity of the Nile Valley with five basic assertions:

1. Sudan is a geographical extention of Egypt.
2. Sudan and Egypt had been linked closely since ancient times.
3. Politically, Sudan had been part of Egypt for some sixty-five years and its boundaries had been established in this period of Turco-Egyptian rule.
4. Sudan and Egypt were similar in language (Arabic), religion (Muslims and some Christians), and ethnic composition.
5. Sudan was re-conquered in 1898 in the name of Egypt, which had supplied most of the funds and troops.[3]

Unlike the Turco-Egyptian period, in which close relations had existed between Sudan and Egypt, the years of the condominium did little to improve those ties. The territorial expansion of the Sudan brought new ethnic groups within its frontiers and the British encouraged Christianity, especially in the south, while thwarting efforts at Arabization there. These conditions placed difficulties in the way of the call for the unity of the Nile Valley. Early Sudanese nationalist movements, such as the White Flag League, however, adopted the unity of the Nile Valley theme. After the

---

3. See, for example, Djam'iat al-Muhandiseen al-Malakkiah al-Misriah, <u>Madjmo'at Muhadrat 'n Wuhadat Wadi al-Niel</u>, (Cairo 1947), and Egypt Council of Ministers, <u>Bianat al-Nikrashi Fi Madjlis al-Amn</u> (Cairo, 1947).

assassination of the British Governor-General of the Sudan, Sir Lee Stack, in Cairo on November 20, 1924, the White Flag provoked a military confrontation with British troops in Khartoum. The British forces finally suppressed the uprising, known in Sudan as the 1924 Revolution.

In the wake of these events, the British authorities acted to minimize Egyptian influence in the Sudan. Almost immediately, Lord Allenby, Britain's High Commissioner in Cairo, sent an ultimatum to the Egyptian Prime Minister threatening the unlimited use of the Nile waters in the Sudan if Egypt did not apologize, pay compensation, bring the assassins of Stack to trial, and cease "anti-British activity". Known Sudanese nationalist leaders were jailed, exiled, or executed; Egyptian teachers and troops were expelled from the Sudan; and restrictions were placed on travel between the two countries. Britain further consolidated its position in the Sudan by establishing a Sudan "defence force" to fill the military vacuum resulting from the expulsion of Egyptian troops; strengthening "native administration"; enhancing economic relations between Sudan and Britain; and attempting to revive the essentially anti-Egyptian Mahdist movement under the leadership of Abdel Rahman al-Mahdi.

Anglo-Egyptian relations remained strained throughout much of the 1920s and 1930s, not least because of the co-domini's differing views on the issue of sovereignty over the Sudan. Egypt insisted on specific rights in the Sudan, couched again in the slogan "Unity of the Nile Valley", but Britain resisted this view. By 1936 the international situation had compelled the two nations to compromise and in August of that year they signed a "Treaty of Friendship and Alliance", article eleven of which dealt with the Sudan question. It introduced no major amendments to the 1899 Agreement, nor did it diminish the Governor-General's powers. Egyptian troops and teachers were, however, permitted to return to the Sudan, and with them came a revival, albeit limited, of Egyptian influence. Nevertheless, the 1936 treaty was one of several factors encouraging the revival of the Sudanese national movement. The exclusion of the Sudanese from any participation in framing the treaty was a major irritant to such educated Sudanese nationalists as Mohamed Ahmed Mahgoub, who wrote:

> To us in Khartoum the sting lay in the parts of the Agreement concerning the Sudan. In these provisions, Britain and Egypt formalized the Condominium, turning what had been an administrative arrangement concocted in 1899 into a longer-term constitutional imposition. In 1899, the system was pressed on us in the name of Britain and Egypt, but in fact under British direction. In 1936, the system was perpetuated with Egypt's official approval. It is true that the 1936 Agreement avoided the thorny problem of sovereignty over the Sudan, but the Sudanese were not invited to take part in the negotiations leading to the Agreement, nor were their views sought. We were deeply hurt.[4]

The growing consciousness of the Sudanese nationalists led to the establishment of the Graduates' General Congress in 1938. The Congress, under the presidency of Ismail El-Azhari, grouped together individuals of widely divergent ideologies and, in the beginning,

---

4. Mohamed Ahmed Mahgoub, Democracy on Trial London 1974), pp. 38-39.

concentrated on the spread of education and social activity, turning to politics after 1942. The willingness of the British authorities in the Sudan to sanction the GGC led Egypt to suspect it of nationalist objectives.

In February 1941, during visit to Khartoum by Egyptian Prime Minister Ali Mahir, the GGC presented him with a memorandum suggesting certain areas for Egyptian-Sudanese cooperation. It urged

> Egyptian philanthropic societies and organizations to establish an Islamic mission in Southern Sudan which would not only be concerned with conversion but also with education and health; to assist the Omdurman Piastre Orphanage with teachers and school materials; to assist in the development of Omdurman's Mahad Ilmi; to encourage Egyptian businessmen to invest capital in the Sudan; to establish a public library in Omdurman; and to establish a modern hospital in Omdurman.[5]

A year later the GGC submitted a memorandum to the Governor-General of the Sudan demanding, among other things, self-determination. The British authorities attributed this demand to the new relationship developing between the GGC and Egypt as the latter's suspicions about the Congress decreased markedly. The demand was immediately rejected, but the GGC's political attitude could not be ignored. To minimize its potential damage, the British promoted sectarianism, personified by Abdel Rahman al-Mahdi of the Ansar and Ali al-Mirghani of the Khatmiyya, and also created an "Advisory

---

5. Mohamed Omer Beshir, Revolution and Nationalism in the Sudan, (London 1974), pp. 157-158. Omdurman received special attention because mahdists (Ansar) were concentrated there.

Council for Northern Sudan" in 1943. These steps aimed at insulating the Sudan's political development from Egypt.

GGC political activity did not, however, cease. In 1945 its executive committee demanded the Congress' representation in any future negotiations concerning the Sudan. Later in the same year the GGC clarified its interpretation of self-determination, saying, this concept meant the formation of a democratic Sudanese government united with Egypt under the Egyptian crown. Not all of the graduates shared this view and two groups, one pro-Egyptian, the other anti-Egyptian and pro-British soon emerged.

Relations After the Second World War

The post-war period witnessed the consolidation of the principle of self-determination throughout the world, but in the Sudan the growing Anglo-Egyptian rivalry made a mockery of this ideal. The problems posed by Egypt's rapidly growing population prompted some of the country's leaders to regard Sudan as an outlet for surplus population and a market for Egyptian products.[6] For the promotion of these goals, and to safeguard its traditional interests in the Nile waters, Egyptian politicians formulated a clear policy towards the Sudan which emphasized historical, cultural, and economic connections. Generating a pro-Egyptian attitude in the Sudan was deemed essential, and education, diplomacy, and public relations were all employed towards that end. For Britain, on the other hand, the Sudan became increasingly more important as a source of cheap raw materials and a market for British products; as a base for the protection of British interests

---

6. L.A. Fabunmi, The Sudan in Anglo-Egyptian Relations 1800-1956. (London 1960), p. 88.

elsewhere, especially in East Africa; and as a buffer to the spread of national consciousness outside Egypt.[7] Like Egypt, Britain introduced new methods and techniques to further its interests.

The competition between the co-domini produced an alternative slogan to "Unity of the Nile Valley" - "Sudan for the Sudanese", a call for the complete independence of the Sudan from both Britain and Egypt. Its proponents asserted that all colonized peoples desired complete independence and only the exceptional circumstances of the condominium had led some Sudanese to call for unity with Egypt. They further maintained that the "Unity of the Nile Valley" would compromise the distinct Sudanese character, whereas independence would enable the Sudanese to exploit fully their country's potential, eventually becoming self-sufficient. Egypt's failure to specify the mechanisms for unity and the precise form it would take, increased Sudanese suspicions about Egypt's desire to dominate the Sudan.[8] In these circumstances, the divisions within the GGC developed into proper political parties classified as: Unionist or Independence.

Not surprisingly, the co-domini responded differently to the two groups. Egypt cooperated with the unionists and viewed the independence parties as separatists created and encouraged by the British. Conversely, Britain favored the latter group, seeing the unionists as Egyptian agents. Anglo-Egyptian jockeying for

---

7. Ibid, p. 89.

8. The Umma Party, Mogarunna Bain El-Istiglal Wa El-Itihad, El-Risala El-Thalitha (Khartoum 1953), p.3.

the support of the Sudanese political parties lessened somewhat with the signing of the Sudan protocol (popularly referred to as the Bevin-Sidky protocol) on 25 October 1946. In its words:

> The policy which the High Contracting Parties undertake to follow in the Sudan (within the framework of unity between the Sudan and Egypt under the common Crown of Egypt) will have for its essential objectives to assure the wellbeing of the Sudanese, the development of their interests, and their active preparation for self-Government and consequently the exercise of the right to choose the future status of the Sudan. Until the High Contracting Parties can in full common agreement realize this latter objective after consultation with the Sudanese, the Agreement of 1899 will continue and Article II of the Treaty of 1936.....[9]

This document reflected the two powers' desire to dominate the Sudan. While endorsing Egyptian sovereignty over the Sudan, it also recognized the right of the Sudanese to choose their future status. Egypt's wish to ensure sovereignty was balanced by Britain's insistence on the continuation of the 1899 agreement and the 1936 treaty.

Ultimately the protocol was variously interpreted in Britain, Egypt, and the Sudan. The independence parties formed an "independence-front" to protest against it to the British government. On the other hand, the unionists were unenthusiastic about backing the protocol, owing to its vagueness. The Egyptian

---

9. Egypt Council of Ministers, Sudan Under New Agreement (Cairo, 1953), p. 33.

parliament rejected the agreement and Mahmoud Fahmi el-Nukrashy succeeded Ismail Sidky as Prime Minister. The new government's efforts to re-negotiate the document failed and it submitted its case against the British presence in the Sudan to the UN Security council in 1947.[10] In the Security Council discussions which followed the Egyptian government demanded "the total and immediate evacuation of British troops from Egypt, including the Sudan ... (and) the termination of the present administrative regime of Sudan".[11] British lobbying efforts, the activity of the Sudanese independence front, and domestic Egyptian opposition all contributed to Egypt's failure to resolve the case satisfactorily in the world forum.

---

10. In his message to the UN Secretary-General on 13 July 1947, El-Nukrashy Pasha expressed the Egyptian case as follows:

    The unwarranted occupation of Egypt by British troops since 1882 and, as a consequence, their occupation of the Southern part of the Nile Valley, the Sudan, have enabled the Government of the United Kingdom, since 1899, to force upon Egypt their partnership in the administration of the Sudan and subsequently to assume exclusive authority therein.

    Taking advantage of the situation, they have adopted a policy designed to sever the Sudan from Egypt, discrediting Egypt and the Egyptians, creating discord between them and the Sudanese and dissention among the Sudanese themselves, instigating and encouraging separatist movements.

    Through this policy, the Government of the United Kingdom has endeavoured and is endeavouring to impair the unity of the Nile Valley, notwithstanding that this unity is urged by the common interests and aspirations of its people.

11. UN Security Council, <u>Verbatim Records of the Discussion of the 175th, 176th, 179th and 182nd of the Security Council</u> (New York 1947), p. 1.

Thereafter, Anglo-Egyptian relations deteriorated, especially as Great Britain began to prepare the Sudan for self-government. In 1948 an ordinance was passed issuing Sudanese nationality. In the same year the British inaugurated a Legislative Assembly which, unlike the previous Advisory Council, represented the whole Sudan, but in which only the independence parties agreed to participate. In December, 1950 the Legislative Assembly passed a proposal expressing Sudan's interest in, and capacity for, self-government and requesting the Governor-General to "approach the Condominium powers with a request that a joint declaration be made... so that the next election to the Assembly may be held on this basis".[12] This resolution provoked fears in Egypt, where it was assumed to be British rather than Sudanese in origin - an assumption, buttressed by the absence of unionist support.

On 16 October 1951 the Egyptian government unilaterally cancelled the 1899 agreement and the 1936 treaty, simultaneously proclaiming King Faruq of Egypt king of the Sudan as well. There followed an announcement that A Sudanese Constituent Assembly would prepare a special constitution for the Sudan with the consent of the king. In Sudan, the Independence parties, led by the Umma, vigorously protested the Egyptian action and even gave

---

12. Sudan Ministry of Interior, <u>Sudan Monthly Record. November-December 1950</u> (Khartoum 1951), pp. 2-3.

some thought to declaring their country's independence.[13] Neither were the Sudanese unionists satisfied. They appreciated the cancellation of the 1899 agreement and the 1936 treaty, but not the installation of Faruq as king of both Egypt and the Sudan. Britain accused Egypt of violating the 1899 agreement and the 1936 treaty, declaring that both remained in effect. Under the guidance and supervision of the Governor-General, however, the Sudan did proceed towards self-government. On 2nd April 1952 the Legislative Assembly passed a "Self-Government Statute", in accordance with which general elections were planned.

In the meantime, political instability prevailed in Egypt, as reflected in many rapid cabinet changes. On 23 July 1953 the Egyptian army, led by Major General Mohammed Neguib, seized power and a "Revolutionary Command Council" took over the management of the state. Political changes in Egypt inevitably led to altered attitudes and relations with the Sudan and as the monarchy gave way to a republican system, Sudanese-Egyptian relations entered a new phase.

---

13. Sir James Robertson, Transition in Africa (London 1974), p. 147. Robertson, then the Civil Secretary noted:

> I have been told on credible authority that as soon as the Egyptian action was known in Omdurman Sayed Abdel Rahman El-Mahdi was pressed by many of his followers to take advantage of the end of the Condominium to declare the Sudan independent, and it was only the opposition of Abdulla Bey Khalil and one or two others which prevented his attempting to stage such a coup. Abdulla Bey is said to have told the Sayed that he had promised Sir James Robertson that the Umma Party would take no unconstitutional action, and this apparently brought Abdel Rahman and his hot-heads back to reality.

THE DYNAMICS OF SELF-RULE

In the Sudan news of Egypt's "July revolution" met with some scepticism and misunderstandings, but the new Egyptian leadership soon overcame these difficulties and contacts were quickly re-established. Instrumental in this process was General Neguib himself. Neguib had been born in Khartoum North in 1901, was of mixed Sudanese-Egyptian ancestry, and had lived in the Sudan for several years. These connections facilitated his access, and that of his colleagues, to Sudanese politicians.

Shortly after coming to power, Egyptian officers sought a solution to the Sudan question. At first they adopted the policy of the unity of the Nile Valley, pursuing it in the same manner as had the previous Egyptian parties. However, after preliminary discussions with Britain, their administrative partner in the Sudan, they became convinced that such a policy would not succeed. The British refused to recognize Egypt's claims, standing firm against any change in the status of the Sudan without consultation with the Sudanese. Consequently, the Revolution Command Council reworked its Sudan policy, striving now to win the support of the Sudanese and to make them allies. In Neguib's words:

> In order to win the sympathy of the Sudanese, with whom we desire the closest of friendly relations, it was necessary to demonstrate that we had nothing in common with the oppressive regimes that had misruled the Nile Valley in the past. The Sudanese were ready to co-operate with us in expelling the British from our common valley, but they had no desire to exchange British for Egyptian masters.

> We had to convince them, as well as some of our other Arab neighbours, that the aggrandizement of Egypt at their expense was not part of our revolutionary programme.[14]

With this in mind, a new Egyptian policy towards the Sudan emerged, grounded in the separation of the Sudan question from other issues relating directly to Egypt (such as the future of the Suez canal and the evacuation of British troops) and the recognition of the Sudanese peoples' right to self-determination. These principles presented a significant reversal, no previous Egyptian government had agreed to separate the Sudan question from purely Egyptian concerns, while the recognition of the Sudanese right to self-determination could be interpreted as an undertaking not to oppose measures already taken by British authorities in the Sudan.

Egypt lost no time in implementing this new policy. Major Salah Salem, a member of the Revolution Command Council, was appointed Minister for National Guidance and Sudanese Affairs and new studies on the constitutional development of the Sudan were commissioned. In these circumstances, consultation with various Sudanese political parties became necessary. A delegation representing the independence parties had, in fact, been in Cairo when the army seized power. Although invited by the deposed government of Ali Mahir Pasha, the coup's leaders continued to negotiate with it, reaching a vague gentlemen's agreement emphasizing friendly relations between the two nations. In addition, Egypt and the Umma party signed a joint statement in October 1952 which read:

14. Mohamed Neguib, Egypt's Destiny (London 1955), pp. 190-191.

> Egypt, who believes in freedom and who considered sovereignty over the Nile Valley with its existing boundaries a right to both Sudanese and Egyptians with no discrimination, and who believes in the unity of the Sudan, welcomes full home rule for the Sudanese people and declares that she preserves the right of the Sudanese to sovereignty in their country until the day they determine their future. If they determine their future in complete freedom, we shall respect this decision. Egypt always welcomes the friendship of the brotherly Sudanese in any form they may choose and will co-operate with them in the political, economic and social fields.[15]

This vague declaration, while revealing Egypt's continuing aspirations for unity with the Sudan, represented at the same time the first occasion on which Egypt had both voluntarily discussed sovereignty over the Sudan, as well as approaching the Sudanese independence parties, particularly the Umma party.

The Umma-Egyptian détente spurred cooperation between Egypt and the unionist parties which, due largely to the efforts of Major Salah Salem, formed a single "National Unionist party" whose creation was announced in Cairo within twenty-four hours of the release of the Egypt-Umma statement. Ismail El-Azhari, the president of the Ashigga party, presided over the new entity, which consisted of the liberals, the unionists, the National Front, and his own party, and which also had the support of the Khatmiyya.

---

15. Abd El-Fattah Ibrahim Baddour, Sudanese-Egyptian Relations, (The Hague, 1960), p. 154.

In this rapidly changing environment, the Egyptian government decided to negotiate with Britain once more. On 2 November 1952 it submitted an official note to the British government requesting the opening of talks on the Sudan question. The note requested the inauguration of a transitional period in which the Sudanese would acquire self-government and which would "provide the requisite free and neutral atmosphere for the Sudanese to exercise Self-Determination".[16] A few days later, the representatives of the Sudanese parties still in Cairo held a press-conference at which they described the contents of the Egyptian note as constituting their minimum demands and threatened to boycott elections in the Sudan and appeal to the UN.[17] The British government believed that a basis for Anglo-Egyptian negotiations now existed and agreed to begin discussions on 20 November 1952 in Cairo. Both sides clearly desired to reach an agreement.

During the negotiations Egypt, represented by key members of the RCC, strove to minimize British influence in the Sudan, while the British delegates, led by the British ambassador to Cairo, focused on preventing Egyptian penetration southward. Both sides claimed to represent the Sudanese people. The Egyptians stressed the need to decrease the powers of the Governor-General of the Sudan, preserve the unity of northern and southern Sudan, and accelerate Sudanization. The British emphasized the need for a joint statement recognizing the right of the Sudanese to self-determination, an agreement on early general elections in the

---

16. Egypt, Council of Ministers, op. cit., p.1.

17. Al-Ahram: 7 November 1952, p.1.

country, and specific safeguards for the south. Differences on many of these issues, especially the necessity of consulting the Sudanese, brought the talks to a halt within a few weeks.

Bowing to British insistence that the co-domini were bound to discuss matters with the Sudanese, Major Salah Salem flew to Khartoum in January 1953. His visit resulted in an agreement signed by the leaders of the Umma party, the NUP, the socialist Republican Party and the Nationalist Party expressing a unified Sudanese view regarding the points still at issue in the British-Egyptian negotiations. The agreement of the parties was an important fact, for it was the first time the NUP and the independence parties had acted jointly. The parties also threatened to boycott any elections held under any statute other than the Self-Government Statute.

The Anglo-Egyptian negotiations resumed shortly afterwards, coming to a final agreement on 12 February 1953.

The most salient points of this accord may be outlined as follows:

1. Both co-domini recognized the Sudan's right to self-determination. A transitional period, not to exceed three years, was specified for self-government. Accordingly, a sudanese cabinet and a parliament were, after general elections, to shoulder the responsibilities of state along with the Governor-General (Articles 1 and 2).
2. A Five-Member Commission would share the powers of the Governor-General (Articles 3, 4, 5, and 6) and Annex I).
3. Procedures to facilitate and govern the conduct of general elections and Sudanization were established

(Articles 7 and 8 and Annexes II and III).

4. The Sudanese parliament could decide on a convenient date for self-determination. The parliament would choose either complete independence for the Sudan or unity with Egypt (Articles 9, 10, 11, 12, 13 and 14, and Annex IV).

Because the condominium powers had to act together to reach the agreement, after a series of unilateral undertakings, it became easier for Egypt to negotiate other outstanding questions with Britain. The agreement received an enthusiastic reception in Egypt, Britain, and the Sudan. It was, however, British diplomacy which had triumphed. Egypt had recognized the right of the Sudan to self-determination after years of having considered no other status for the Sudan other than its being part of Egypt. The Governor-General also remained quite powerful.[18] Finally, although the Sudan could choose unity with Egypt or complete independence, the agreement detailed the procedures to be followed even after the Sudan had achieved self-determination. These procedures were oriented towards Sudanese independence, not unity with Egypt.

Nevertheless, the Egyptians believed the agreement would result in unity with the Sudan. The overconfidence of the country's leaders blinded them to the potential impact of new factors which might arise during the transitional period. Neguib, for example, expressed his conviction that "democracy and a free referendom for the people of the Sudan would give the same

---

18. Article 3 of the Agreement stated that "The Governor-General shall, during the transitional period, be the Supreme constitutional Authority within the Sudan".

result - the unity of the people of the Nile Valley".[19]

The Establishment of Self-Rule

Within hours after the agreement's signing, however, a new battle had been joined, as the British Prime Minister told the House of Commons that

> Complete independence does not exclude the right of any country to apply, if it wishes, for association with or membership of the British Commonwealth, or indeed to make any other arrangements it so wishes which are in accord with its complete independence.[20]

The Egyptian authorities reacted immediately and violently against the statement, for it brought to their minds the different interpretations attached to the Sidki-Bevin protocol in 1946. The silence of the Umma party increased Egyptian suspicions that it was collaborating with the British, and the Egyptian government emphasized that the recently concluded document left room for only two options for the Sudan: independence (with no Commonwealth link) or unity with Egypt. In view of the fact that Commonwealth membership had been under consideration since 1951, Egypt's reaction appeared rather extreme. The British statement was, however, an attempt to strengthen the independence option by reminding the Sudanese that membership in the Commonwealth would not deprive it of its sovereignty as the unity of the Nile Valley scheme would. To emphasize the continuity of British policy towards

---

19. Mohammed Neguib, Kulimaty Lil Tareech (Beirut 1972), p. 77.

20. House of Commons, Parliamentary Debates. Fifth Series, Vol. DXI, Session 1952-1953, p. 160.

the Sudan even after the agreement, the Governor-General continued in office until 1955.

Self-rule was accelerated by the formation of the Governor-General's Commission, the passage of the Selt-Government Statute, the holding of elections, and the process of Sudanization. Created in February 1953, the commission consisted of a Pakistani, an Egyptian, a Briton, and two Sudanese. To ensure a neutral political atmosphere for self-determination, the Pakistani member assumed the chairmanship of the commission, with two Sudanese on the commission, however, the representation of the country's interest was guaranteed.

On March 21, 1953, the Governor-General issued a "Self-Government Statute", closely parallelling the existing Self-Government Ordinance, which more or less became the constitution of self-rule. It was to remain in effect until the Governor-General declared the institution of self-government complete. The statute laid down detailed procedures and regulations for the establishment and operations of the organs of government, very much reflecting the British parliamentary system. Sudan's parliament was to have two chambers, a House of Representatives and a Senate with the Prime Minister elected from the House and his cabinet collectively responsible to Parliament. This British model inevitably influenced the course of self-determination.

The Governor-General also appointed a mixed electoral commission consisting of an Indian chairman, an Egyptian, a Briton. an American. and three Sudanese, representing the major political groupings (the NUP, the Umma Party, and the southern Sudan). The southern Sudan had never before been represented as a political group and its inclusion testified to the realization of the Sudan's imbalanced socio-economic development and a desire to compensate for previous neglect. The American presence on the commission underscored the reduced power of post-war Britain and the consequent need to encourage American involvement.

Although it had been hoped to hold early elections, the approach of Ramadan and the rainy season forced a delay until November and December. The elections were contested in two categories - geographical constituencies and the graduates' constituency.

The election results, announced on December 20, 1953, showed a clear success for the Unionists, with NUP winning 83 of the 147 seats, including all those of Khartoum Province. The independence parties suffered a strong defeat - the Umma secured thirty seats and the Anti-Imperialist front only one and the other parties took only a handful of seats (see Table 1). Thus, the UNP was in a strong position to form a government.

There were widely differing reactions to the election results in the Sudan, Egypt, and Britain. The Sudanese independence parties, led by the Umma, refused to accept the results as a final victory for the unity with Egypt forces. Rather, the Umma laid the groundwork for another competition with the Unionists,. In a strong statement to the BBC after the announcement of the results of the geographical constituencies, El-Sideeq el-Mahdi, the Umma President, accused Egypt of meddling in the elections.

> One of the reasons behind the result was the intensive and severe intervention of Egypt and its propaganda by various means, thus misleading the voters. Accordingly, the neutral voters were influenced. In turn they voted in favour of Unionists, while it was natural that they should have voted in favour of the advocates of complete independence.[21]

21. <u>Al-Umma</u>, Khartoum, December 10, 1953.

The complainants produced no solid evidence of Egyptian intervention and the UNP proceeded to form the first Sudanese government.

Egypt denied these charges, attributing the success of the NUP, which the Egyptians interpreted as a guarantee of unity, to the recently altered political situation in Egypt. In Neguib's world,

> previous Egyptian Governments had failed to win the support of a majority of the Sudanese because of their insistance on the tutelege of a hated Egyptian monarchy. The Egyptian Republic easily won the majority's support because it was willing to recognize Sudan's right to independence even though it continued to advocate the principle of unity. The Sudanese knew that the new Egypt, while eager to unify the Nile Valley, was prepared to deal with the new Sudan on a basis of equality.[22]

During this time, the British authorities remained silent, keeping their policy towards the Sudan unchang ed - independence as the minimum British objective.

The inauguration of the Sudanese parliament on January 1, 1954 saw the translation of the NUP's overwhelming majority into concrete terms as its supporters became speakers of both chambers: Babikir Awadalla in the House of Representatives, Ahmed Mohamed Yassein in the Senate. On January 6, the House elected the NUP president, Ismail El-Azhari, Prime Minister; two days later he, in turn, submitted the list of his cabinet mdmbers, all NUP members, to the Governor-General. In addition to El-Azhari as both Prime Minister and Minister of the Interior, the Cabinet included Mohamed Nur El-Din (Minister of Works), Mirghani Hamza (Minister of

---

22.Mohamed Neguib, op. cit., p. 247.

Table No. 1.
Results of the Sudanese General Elections of 1953.

A) The House of Representatives:

Province	NUP	Umma	SRP	Ind.	SP	FAC	Total
Blue Nile	6	10	2	–	–	–	18
Dar Fur	2	6	1	2	–	–	11
Northern	7	–	–	–	–	–	7
Bahr el-Ghazal	2	–	–	4	1	–	7
Equatoria	–	–	–	3	4	–	7
Upper Nile	4	–	–	2	2	–	8
Kassala	7	1	–	–	–	–	8
Khartoum	9	–	–	–	–	–	9
Kordofan	11	6	–	–	–	–	17
Graduates	3	–	–	1	–	1	5
TOTAL	51	23	3	12	7	1	97

B) The Senate:

Province	UNP	Umma	SRP	Ind.	SP	FAC	Total
Blue Nile	4	1	–	–	–	–	5
Dar Fur	2	1	–	1	–	–	4
Northern	3	–	–	–	–	–	3
Bahr el-Ghazal	1	–	–	1	1	–	3
Equatoria	1	–	–	–	1	–	2
Upper Nile	2	–	–	–	1	–	3
Kassala	3	–	–	–	–	–	3
Khartoum	2	–	–	–	–	–	2
Kordofan	4	1	–	–	–	–	5
Graduates	10	4	1	4	1	–	20
TOTAL	32	7	1	6	4	–	50

(1) Sudan Ministry of Interior, Sudan Monthly Record. No.276, November-December 1953 (Khartoum, 1953), p.1.

Agriculture, Education, and Irrigation), Hammad Towfik (Minister of Finance), Ibrahim El-Mufti (Minister of Economics), Mubarak Zarroug (Minister of Communications), Khalafalla Khalid (Minister of Defence), Ali Abdel Rahman (Minister of Justice), Dr. Amin Es-Sayed (Minister of Health), Bullen Alier (Minister without Portfolio; then Minister of Animal Production), Dak Dei (Minister without Portfolio), and Sentino Deng (Minister without Portfolio). No Ministry of Foreign Affairs was established, since the agreement left this realm within the responsibility of the Governor-General. The various parties which had amalgamated to form the UNP were rewarded with ministerial appointments, while the independence parties were not invited to participate. To encourage the cooperation of southern Sudanese, three of their number were included in the Cabinet.

The Prime Minister invited General Neguib and Mr Selwyn Lloyd, the British Secretary of State, to atend the opening session of Parliament on March 1, 1954. When the Egyptian delegation arrived at Khartoum airport, it was met by Ansar demonstrators gathered by the Umma party. The Governor-General declared a state of emergency in the province of Khartoum and the inaugural session of Parliament was postponed until March 10, to forestall any further loss of lives or property. Neguib returned to Cairo on the following day. The March Incidents, as they became to be known, marked the beginning of a new phase of relations between Egypt, the NUP, and the Umma party. They gave proof of the threat of civil war if unity with Egypt materialized.

Even before the formal opening of the Parliament an eight member Sudanization committee was established. It devoted its initial efforts to those public positions considered most likely to hinder the emergence of the neutral political climate required for self-determination. These included, most notably, the police and the Sudan Defence force. In April 1954 the Governor General appointed a Public Service Commission to complement the Sudanization Committee by making recommendations to the ministers on the recruitment, appointment , promotion, transfer, and retirement of government employees.

In August, Parliament decided to evacuate all Egyptian and British troops, thereby creating a cacuum which only the Sudan Defence Force could fill. Major-General Ahmed Mohamed replaced the British Major-General R.L. Scoones as commander of the force at the end of November, at which time the last foreign soldiers left Khartoum.

In June 1955, the Governor-General amended the terms of the original agreement to allow the recruitment of individuals who were neither British nor Egyptian to fill posts scheduled for Sudanization but for which no qualified Sudanese were available. As a result, many Indians, Pakistanis, and others replaced British and Egyptian officials in the Sudan administration. Two months later the Sudanization Committee announced the completion of its work. In its final report to the Governor-General the committee noted that it had reviewed 1222 posts, 1069 of which British citizens had held, while Egyptians filled only 153. Although Egypt had believed that Sudanization would hasten the unity of the Nile Valley, this proved not to be so. Instead, Sudanese citizens of British educational background, in favour of complete independence for the Sudan, came to lead the government. These men quickly proceeded along the path of self-determination.

Self Determination

Within weeks of the Sudanization committee's report, both chambers of Parliament passed a motion which stated their wish that "arrangements for self-determination should be put in motion forthwith".[23] The motion, a major victory for the independence parties, revealed the decreasing influence of the unionists. Since the opening of Parliament in early 1954 many factors had served to undermine the unionist movement.

One of these was the replacement of General Neguib by Colonel Nasser in November, 1954. Beginning in the previous March, the Revolutionary Command Council had begun shunting Neguib to the sidelines. As these manoevres became public, some of the Sudanese unionists, fearful of their implications for the Sudan, attempted to mediate between Neguib and Nasser. These efforts failed, however, and Neguib's ousting signalled the erosion of a strong link between the Sudanese and Egyptian leadership.[24] Nasser lacked Neguib's contacts with the Sudan, knowing the country primarily through his service there with the Egyptian army between 1939 and 1942. In the Nasser era, Egypt focused increasingly on external affairs. The Sudan occupied only a small place in the expanding realm of Egyptian foreign policy, and the special position which Neguib had envisaged for the Sudan vanished.

---

23. Parliament of Sudan, Weekly Digest of Proceedings in the House of Representatives, No.8, Third Session (Khartoum, 1955).

24. El-Dirdiri Mohamed Osman, Mozukkirati (1914-1958), Khartoum, 1961), p. 62.

Political intrique also undermined the strength of the unionists. As some of its members embarked on public criticisms of party policy towards Egypt, the NUP lost cohesion and the groups which had joined to form the party reasserted themselves. Eventually even the sectarian support of the Khatmiyya was no longer assurred. In December 1954, El-Azhari dismissed two ministers, enlarged and reshuffled his cabinet, and assumed for himself the duties of the Interior and Defence Ministries.

As the unionists weakened, the independence movement grew more confident. In January, 1955, an "independence front" consisting of the Umma, the Socialist Republican party, the Republican party and the Anti-Imperialism front emerged. It advocated the complete independence of the Sudan, the preservation of public freedom and opposition to any military alliance or foreign aid that might affect the Sudan's sovereignty.

During the summer of 1955, civil war broke out in the southern Sudan, beginning with the mutiny of the Equatoria corps. In many ways the war aided the "in dependence front". For one thing, it strengthened the identification of the southern Sudanese as a distinct political group, leading to their later call for the establishment of a federal state. In adopting this position, the southerners were effectively eschewing any concept of unity with Egypt. Moreover, the NUP was in power when the war erupted and was saddled with the blame for the insecurity which followed the severe suppression of the mutiny. When the Sudanese government appealed only to the Governor-General for assistance, misunderstanding and tensions grew between the NUP and Egypt, and Cairo began a reconsideration of its relations with the Sudan.

In the Sudan the opposition pressed for the creation of a national government. On November 10, the House of Representatives passed a vote of no-confidence against the NUP, but El-Azhari was re-elected Prime Minister a few days later. Cooperation between the rival factions was still necessary. As if to emphasize this point, Abdel Rahman al-Mahdi, the Ansar leader and patron of the Umma Party, and Ali El-Mirghani, the Khatmiyya leader and NUP patron, met for the first time since 1946. On December 4, the two Sayyids issued a joint declaration.

> Now that the great hope of this country has been realized, it gives us pleasure to declare our determination to stand together and co-operate in all that leads the Sudanese people to prosperity and happiness, freedom and full sovereignty.
>
> Our desire that the country should peacefully pass through the critical time ahead until it decides its future makes us appeal to all the people to forget themselves in serving their beloved country and in realizing its great aspirations until the stability and confidence necessary at the present difficult time are restored.
>
> We sincerely hope that all parties will get together immediately to form a national government which will be the safety valve at this difficult time and will protect the country against expected danger.[25]

This statement sanctified co-operation between the political parties, with the formation of a national government as a suitable platform for such co-operation. As a result, the influence of both co-domini

---

25. The Morning News, Khartoum, December 5, 1955, p.1.

diminished greatly.

In the light of these events, Sudanese independence was inevitable. The overwhelming parliamentary majority of the NUP no longer threatened independence, and the southern Sudanese MPs now backed it as well, believing that their demand for federation would be considered later. Thus, on December 19 the House of Representatives unanimously passed a motion declaring that the "Sudan is to become a fully independent sovereign State" and requesting the Governor-General to ask the co-domini to recognize this status. The Senate unanimously passed the same motion three days later. Egypt and Great Britain quickly accepted the Sudan's decision and January 1, 1956 was fixed as independence day. On December 26, Parliament elected a five member committee called the Supreme Council to replace the Governor-General and his Commission.

Independence:

Independence further decreased the unionists' influence. Dissidents from the NUP soon established a new political party, the People's Democratic party, which enjoyed the support of the Khatmiyya. In July, 1956, the Umma party and the PDP formed a coalition government replacing the NUP and the Umma's Secretary General, Abdulla Khalil, became Prime Minister.

In the meantime, Egypt moved to restore friendly relations with the Sudan. It was the first country officially to recognize the independent Sudan and quickly established proper diplomatic representations. In addition to an embassy in Khartoum, Egypt opened consulates in El-Obeid and Port Sudan. Egypt facilitated the Sudan's participation in the Bandung Conference and its admission to the Arab League. In turn, the Sudan raised the status of the Sudan Agency in Cairo (and London) to embassy level.

At the same time, Cairo opposed any Sudanese tendency, real of imagined, towards membership in the Commonwealth in such western alliances as the Baghdad Pact. Having failed in their bid for unity with the Sudan, Egypt's leaders now hoped to keep their southern neighbour non-aligned. Egyptian suspicions of western intervention in the Sudan were another manifestation of the longstanding concern over the possibility of a power hostile to Egypt securing control over the Upper Nile. A desire to nurture anti-western sentiment in this critical area led to a substantial rise in Egyptian aid to African liberation movements in the late 1950s.

The Sudan's Attitude:

Historically, the Sudan had not formulated a specific policy towards Egypt, but contented itself with reacting to Egyptian policies. Several factors explain this passive approach. Less developed than Egypt, the Sudan is more vulnerable to political instability. The Sudan has no intrinsic interest in Egyptian territory, although it views the technical skills and employment opportunities which Egypt provides as quite attractive. Perhaps because Sudanese foreign policy has often been based on personal relations, Sudanese reactions to Egyptian policies have always been inconsistent. El-Azhari himself, for example, told the Egyptian leaders in May, 1955, that "Unity was no longer contemplated by any of the major Sudanese political parties".[26]

No one in the Sudan interpreted independence to mean a break in relations with Egypt - an assumption

26. Tareq Y. Ismael, op. cit., p.18.

which Egypt's conciliatory policy confirmed. Sudanese politicians continued to seek amiable contacts with Egypt, as their support in the Suez crisis illustrated. Nevertheless, Sudanese-Egyptian relations did deteriorate. Serious crises occurred in 1958 over border issues and the Nile waters. The tensions which they provoked lessened, albeit briefly, during the Abboud regime when a Trade and Payment Agreement was concluded in 1959 and a Permanent Joint Technical Commission on the Nile Waters established in the following year. The Sudan's ailing economy contributed to popular discontent regarding Egypt, some of which became quite evident following the 1964 revolution. Internal affairs in each country greatly influenced Sudanese-Egyptian relations. Interests, rather than ideology, have been the principal forces at work.

The need to react to Egyptian moves prevented the Sudanese authorities from concentrating on other key foreign policy issues. The policy of non- alignment continued, but the Sudan did not substantially further its links with Africa. Only civil war prompted an interest in restoring friendly relations with its neighbours, supporting the struggle against colonialism and racial discrimination, and promoting African cooperation through the OAU. On the other hand, the Sudan's relations with the Arab world had been influenced by the pattern of its relations with Egypt.

Further Sudanese- Egyptian relations will continue to depend heavily on matters involving the Nile waters. Although the 1959 agreement averted a potential conflict, the Sudan has challenged it on several occasions. Egyptian-Sudanese cooperation in the Jonglei canal project, and the benefits which the scheme offers both countries, however, suggests that the future may see less tension over this perennial issue.

Indeed, such cooperation is essential for both countries, and may, in the long run, contribute to the prosperity and security of the Arab, African, Islamic, and non-aligned countries alike. If, for instance, the surplus manpower of Egypt along with financial support from Arab oil producing states were employed in developing the uncultivated but fertile land of the Sudan, vast quantities of food could be grown for Third World consumption. Success in these kinds of joint ventures depends upon allaying the Sudan's traditional fear of Egyptian domination. This can be achieved by stressing projects of mutual interest. The intensification of technical assistance; frequent consultations on and coordination of foreign policy issues; the opening of adequate channels for the exchange of information; and the resolution of differences by direct negotiations all means of promoting successful collaboration. The sine qua non in all this, however, is complete respect for the sovereignty of each state.

In substituting cooperation for unity, economic and and cultural links become an end in themselves rather than simply means for attaining other goals. Arabization, education, population movements, and economic co-ordination are all desirable. Many challenges still remain on the path to cooperation. The existence of different political, legal and educational institutions reveal the lingering effects of colonialism. Any attempt to bring conformity to these institutions inevitably produces suspicion and fear. Nevertheléws, a carefully thought out formula for cooperation which eliminates the fear of domination and excludes policies designed to benefit one side to the exclusion of the other is not beyond reach and should be the goal of future Sudanese and Egyptian policy.